Berlitz

Paris

Front cover and right: Eiffel Tower

TOP 10 ATTRACTIONS

Centre Pompidou • The inside-out museum showcases art from 1905 to the present day *(page 48)*

Latin Quarter and St-Germain-des-Prés • Once the heart of literary Paris, these districts are a haven of high fashion *(page 67)*

Eiffel Tower • Built for the 1889 World Fair, it is still the most potent symbol of Paris *(page 80)*

Arc de Triomphe • Built to celebrate Napoleon's victories, it dominates the top of the Champs-Elysées *(page 57)*

The Louvre • Once home of kings, now home to the world's most outstanding collection of fine and decorative arts *(page 36)*

Montmartre • Artistic heritage, lively bars and some of the most romantic streets in the city – this celebrated hill has them all *(page 62)*

Jardin du Luxembourg • Relax in the quintessential Paris park *(page 75)*

Musée d'Orsay • A treasure trove of fine art from 1848 to 1919, notably some outstanding Impressionist works *(page 76)*

Place des Vosges • One of the most elegant squares in Paris *(page 52)*

Notre-Dame • A monument to Catholicism and the great Gothic architects *(page 28)*

A PERFECT DAY

8.00am Breakfast

Ask your hotel concierge for directions to the nearest good boulangerie. Once there, buy some still-warm croissants or pains au chocolat and find a leafy square nearby to eat them in.

9.00am Boat tour

Begin at the city's origin, the River Seine. Make your way to the western tip of the Ile-de-la-Cité, via the steps down from the Pont-Neuf. From here, take one of the Vedettes du Pont-Neuf boat tours – a lovely way to see the city.

10.30am Rue de Seine

From the Pont-Neuf, walk along quai de Conti then amble down characterful rue de Seine with its art and fashion boutiques.

11.00am Coffee break

At the Palais du Luxembourg, turn left and walk along the railings of the famous Jardin du Luxembourg, most elegant of Paris parks. Stop for a strong espresso at the smart café Le Rostand *(see page 114)*, on the square at the garden's eastern tip.

12 noon Park and lunch

After an hour in the Jardin in the company of joggers, boules players, statues and smooching couples, make your way to nearby restaurant La Ferrandaise *(see page 114)* and enjoy a lunch of updated French classics.

IN PARIS

2.30pm Palais Garnier

Walk towards the river along teeming boulevard St-Michel and get the métro to Opéra. Leave the station by the main exit and marvel at the gilded opera house right behind you.

3.30pm Retail therapy

Walk past the Palais Garnier to boulevard Haussmann, and do some shopping in the two vast department stores, Galeries Lafayette (no. 40) and Printemps (no. 64). Return to the square in front of the opera and have another rest and a drink at the historic Café de la Paix *(see page 109)*.

6.00pm Montmartre and dinner

Take the métro to Abbesses, on the hill of Montmartre. Follow your nose through the atmospheric, winding streets, but don't go too far. After dinner at friendly bistro Chez Toinette *(see page 113)*, walk to Sacré-Coeur and savour the panoramic view over the city from its front steps.

9.30pm Bar hopping

Walk downhill to boulevard de Rochechouart and take a taxi to rue Jean-Pierre Timbaud, east of place de la République. This street and those around it teem with trendy bars – the perfect counterpoint to the historic attractions you've seen earlier.

CONTENTS

78

27

64

Features

39

105

56

INTRODUCTION

The fascination of the French capital – the 'city of cities', as Victor Hugo put it – is eternal. For over 2,000 years, it has steadily grown in size and reputation, and each of its many layers is rich in history and intrigue. Unlike many European cities, it was left almost unscathed by the two world wars, and its celebrated streets, monuments and museums still work their centuries-old magic today. And then there's the artistic heritage of the 'City of Light', long a powerhouse of art, literature, music and philosophy. Little wonder that the Parisian is so proud to be part of a city that, according to writer Jean Giraudoux, is home to 'the greatest amount of thinking, talking and writing in the world'.

Culture capital

Despite concerted attempts at decentralisation in France, Paris continues to dominate the country's art, literature, music, fashion, education, scientific research, commerce and politics.

Geography

Situated on longitude 2° 20'W and latitude 48° 50'N, roughly the same latitude as Stuttgart in Germany and Vancouver in Canada, Paris is where all the French channels of communication lead. The city itself covers an area close to 100 sq km (40 sq miles), running 13km (8 miles) east and west, and 9km (6 miles) north and south. On the map, 20 *arrondissements* (administrative districts) spiral out like a snail's shell, a pattern reflecting the city's historical development and successive enlargements.

The River Seine enters Paris close to the Bois de Vincennes in the southeast and meanders gently north and south past three small islands – the Ile St-Louis, Ile de la Cité and, on its

The view towards the Louvre pyramid

The view from Sacré-Coeur

way out, Ile des Cygnes. Chains of hillocks rise up to the north of the river, including Montmartre (the city's highest point), Ménilmontant, Belleville and Buttes Chaumont; and, to the south, Montsouris, the Mont Ste-Geneviève, Buttes aux Cailles and Maison Blanche.

The city is contained by the Périphérique, a ring road stretching 35km (22 miles) around it. Built in 1973 to try to reduce traffic jams, the Périphérique is now invariably congested itself, particularly during rush hours, when around 150,000 cars storm its 35 exits. Forming two concentric rings wrapped tightly around Paris, the suburbs *(la banlieue)* are divided up into *départements* or counties.

At the beginning of the 19th century, Napoleon Bonaparte imposed a special status on the city of Paris, giving it the powers of a *département* in order to maintain a firm hold on the capital's politics and populace. Today, each *arrondissement* also has its own council and mayor to deal with local affairs. Nationally, Paris is represented by 21 delegates and 12 senators in the two houses of the French Parliament.

The River

'Buffeted by the waves but sinks not,' reads the Latin inscription on the city's coat-of-arms, symbolising a Paris born on the flanks of the River Seine. Lutetia (as the city founded by the Romans was called) was established on the site of a Gallic Parisii settlement on the largest island in the river, but today it is the Seine that cuts a swathe through the middle of the city. The Seine is the capital's widest avenue; it is spanned by a total of 37 bridges, which provide some of the loveliest views of Paris.

The river is also the city's calmest thoroughfare, notwithstanding the daily flow of tourist and commercial boat traffic. In the 19th century, the banks were encumbered with wash-houses and watermills, and its waters heaved with ships from every corner of France. Even more difficult to imagine now are the 700 Viking warships that sailed up the river to invade Paris from the north in the 9th century, or the thousands of bodies that floated past in 1572, victims of the St Bartholomew's Day Massacre, turning the Seine into a river of blood. Today, barges and pleasure boats on their way to Burgundy use the St-Martin and St-Denis canals to shorten their trip, cutting across the northeast of the city.

Paris Ambience

One of the most persistent images of Paris is one of long avenues elegantly lined with chestnut and plane trees. Flowers and plants abound in a patchwork of squares, parks and gardens, tended in the formal French tradition or following the English style so admired by Napoleon III. Divided up by two long ribbons of streets, one tracing a long line north to south (from

Cafés are still a vital part of everyday Paris life

An original Art Nouveau Métro entrance at Abbesses

boulevard de Strasbourg to boulevard St-Michel) and the other running from east to west (from rue du Faubourg-St-Antoine as far as La Défense), Paris is a mosaic of *quartiers* (quarters) or 'villages', each one having a distinctive character. Chains of boulevards encircle the centre of the city, marking where the boundary was in medieval times. Several streets contain the word *faubourg*, indicating that they were once part of the suburb outside the city wall.

The most important unofficial division in Paris is between the traditionally working-class eastern end of the city and the mostly bourgeois west. In general, the further east you go, the further left you will find yourself on the political spectrum. Rents are steep in the western *arrondissements* whereas property tends to be more affordable – for the time being – in the east. City planners have been struggling for decades to improve the balance, culminating in massive urban renewal projects at Bercy and the 'new' Left Bank *(see page 73)* in the southeast.

Population

Paris is more densely populated than Tokyo, London or New York, and the Parisians' high stress levels can be partly put down to the fact that they live literally on top of one another, squeezed into small apartments, packed into the city's 100 sq km (40 sq miles). A house and garden is an almost unheard-of luxury. There is intense competition for desirable living space, with an average of 150,000 people looking for a home at any one time. It is an oft-cited paradox that this battle for a place to live occurs in a city where 16 percent of apartments lie vacant. High rents also contribute to the fact that many Parisians have neither the time nor the money to appreciate the city they live in, being trapped in a monotonous routine they describe as *métro-boulot-dodo* (commuting, working, sleeping).

Nonetheless, for anyone fortunate enough to live in the city centre the rewards far outweigh the demands. Human in scale, clean, safe, cosmopolitan and lively, Paris lives up to its reputation as one of the best cities on earth for enjoying the good life.

Café Culture

Cafés have long played a key part in the city's intellectual, political and artistic development. Café Voltaire (1 place de l'Odéon) was where, in the 18th century, Voltaire used to meet fellow philosopher Diderot to discuss their Enlightenment theories. The 19th-century poets Verlaine and Mallarmé also conversed here, and in the 1920s the American writers Ernest Hemingway and F. Scott Fitzgerald extolled the café's 'sudden provincial quality'. Other writers in Paris between the two world wars spent hours at their favourite tables in Le Procope (13 rue de l'Ancienne-Comédie), and the Existentialist writer and philosopher Jean-Paul Sartre and his lover Simone de Beauvoir consolidated the high-brow reputation of Les Deux Magots (6 place St-Germain-des-Prés) in the 1950s. The Art Deco Café de Flore (172 boulevard St-Germain) was another of Sartre's favourites. Today, politicians congregate at Brasserie Lipp across the road.

A BRIEF HISTORY

Paris began as an island fishing community and trading port in the middle of the River Seine. Stone Age inhabitants left the earliest traces (3000BC) on the Right Bank under what is now the Louvre, but it was c.250BC before the town took form under the skilful hands of the Parisii, a Celtic tribe that settled on the Ile de la Cité.

Their island, well away from the banks of the river – much wider and more rapid than today – provided refuge from the fierce Belgae to the east. The Parisii minted their own finely crafted gold coins for trade as far afield as Britain and the Mediterranean, and the town's prosperity and strategic position attracted the attention of Julius Caesar, whose Roman legions conquered it in 52BC.

Roman stonework in the Musée National du Moyen Age

The land bordering the river was marshy (according to some philologists, the town's ancient name Lutetia means 'marshland'), so the Romans extended inland to what is now the Left Bank's Latin Quarter. Rue St-Jacques and rue St-Martin follow the route of the old Roman road linking northern France to Orléans. Scant subterranean masonry has been found from the Roman buildings – forum, theatres, temples – but there are substantial remains of the public baths in what is now a wing of the Musée National du Moyen Age.

Headless martyr

Around AD250 St Denis brought Christianity to Lutetia – much to the displeasure of the Romans, who had him decapitated the hill of Montmartre. According to legend, the martyr picked up his head and walked away with it tucked under his arm.

Huns and Franks overran Roman Gaul in the 3rd century, driving the citizens to retrench in the fortified Ile de la Cité – which was renamed Paris around this time. In 508, Clovis, King of the Franks, set up his court here. He later converted to Christianity, and several religious foundations date from this time – including those of the city's oldest church, St-Germain-des-Prés.

The Capetians

From 845, Norman pirates regularly raided Paris. The city stagnated until 987, when Hugues Capet, Count of Paris, became King of France. His Capetian dynasty went on to make the city the economic and political capital of France. The River Seine was once again the key to commercial prosperity, symbolised by the ship on the city's coat-of-arms with the motto *Fluctuat nec mergitur* ('Buffeted by the waves but does not sink'). The Right Bank port area, known as the Grève, developed around the site of the present-day Hôtel de Ville.

Philippe Auguste (1180–1223) used the revenue from trade to build a fortress called the Louvre (its lower ramparts are clearly visible beneath today's museum), Notre-Dame, paved streets, aqueducts and freshwater fountains. To protect his investment while he was away on the Third Crusade, he surrounded the city with walls.

The profoundly devout, and later canonised, Louis IX (1226–70) gave the city one of its great Gothic masterpieces,

Sainte-Chapelle, and his patronage of spiritual and intellectual life gave rise to the Left Bank's Latin Quarter. From the many new schools frequented by Latin-speaking clerics, the Sorbonne university evolved, established by the king's chaplain, Robert de Sorbon. By the end of Louis's reign Paris was one of the largest cities in Western Christendom, with a population of 100,000.

In the 14th century, the city's merchant class took advantage of the political vacuum left by the devastating Black Death and the Hundred Years War with England. In 1356, with King Jean le Bon held prisoner at Poitiers, the merchants' leader, Etienne Marcel, set up a municipal government in Paris. Although he was assassinated two years later, he had shown that the Parisians were a force to be reckoned with. Wary of their militancy, Jean's successor Charles V built the Bastille fortress.

English Occupation and Religious Conflict

Civil unrest continued unabated. In 1407 the Duke of Burgundy had the Duke of Orléans murdered on rue Barbette, which led to 12 years of strife between their supporters. The Burgundians called in the help of the English, who entered Paris in 1420, following French defeat at Agincourt by England's Henry V. Ten years later, Joan of Arc tried and failed to get the English out, and in the following year came a worse humiliation: Henry VI of England was crowned King of France. But the triumph of the English was short-lived: they were soon expelled from the city, and by 1453 had lost all their French possessions except for Calais.

In the early 16th century, the city thrived under an absolutist and absent monarch, François I (1515–47), who was occupied with wars in Italy, and even imprisoned for a year in Spain. Much of the Louvre was torn down and rebuilt along the present lines. A new Hôtel de Ville (city hall) was begun, as well as the grand St-Eustache church.

The new splendour was soon bloodied by religious war, starting in 1572 with the St Bartholomew's Day massacre of 3,000 Protestants in Paris and culminating in the siege of the city by Henri de Navarre in 1589. Before the Catholic League capitulated, 13,000 Parisians had died of starvation. Henri was crowned at Chartres and finally entered the capital in 1594 – not before having converted to Catholic himself, though his quip 'Paris is well worth a Mass' is almost certainly apocryphal.

Henri IV did Paris proud once he was its master. He built the beautiful place des Vosges and place Dauphine, embellished the banks of the river with the quai de l'Arsenal, quai de l'Horloge and quai des Orfèvres, and even constructed the Samaritaine hydraulic machine that pumped fresh water to Right Bank households until 1813. The most popular of France's monarchs, *le bon roi Henri* (good King Henry) was a notorious ladies' man. He completed the Pont-Neuf (the oldest bridge in Paris) as well as the adjacent gardens, where he was known to dally with his ladies.

The Palais du Luxembourg, built for Henri IV's widow

During the reign of Louis XIII (1610–43), Paris began to take on the fashionable aspect that became its hallmark. Elegant houses sprang up along rue du Faubourg-St-Honoré, and the magnificent *hôtels* (mansions) of the nobility were constructed in the Marais. The capital strengthened its hold on the country with the founding of a royal printing press and Cardinal Richelieu's Académie Française.

Paris increasingly attracted nobles from the provinces – although too many for the liking of Louis XIV, *le Roi Soleil* ('the Sun King', 1643–1715). To bring his overly powerful and independent aristocrats into line, Louis decided to move the court out to Versailles, compelling the courtiers to live at ruinous expense in his enormous new palace.

Paris lost some of its political importance, but looked more impressive than ever, with the landscaping of the Jardin des Tuileries and the Champs-Elysées, and the building of the Louvre's great colonnade and the Invalides hospital for wounded soldiers. The city asserted a leading cultural position in Europe with its new academies of the arts, literature and sciences and the establishment of the Comédie Française (1680) and several other theatres. By this time, the population had increased to 560,000.

The rumble of popular discontent grew louder however, as corruption and heavy taxes for costly foreign wars marked the reigns of the Sun King's successors, the languid Louis XV (1715–74) and the inept Louis XVI (1774–93). One of the final construction projects of the *ancien régime*

Maximilien de Robespierre

was a 23-km (14-mile) wall encircling the city. Begun in 1784, it was a key factor in the subsequent unrest, for at points along the wall taxes were collected on goods brought into the city.

The Revolution

Paris was the epicentre of the political earthquake that was the French Revolution, whose aftershocks spread across France to shake up a whole continent. It had all started with protests about taxes and turned into an assault on the privileges of the monarchy, the aristocracy and the church. Middle-class intellectuals made common cause with the urban poor, the previously powerless *sans-culottes* (literally, people without breeches) to revolt. The revolutionaries destroyed the prison-fortress of the Bastille on 14 July 1789, and proceeded to execute the perceived enemies of the new republic.

A climax was reached on 21 January 1793, with the public beheading of Louis XVI. In the Reign of Terror later that year, several revolutionaries followed Louis to the guillotine: Camille Desmoulins, the fiery orator; Danton, who tried to moderate the Terror; and then the men who had organised it, Robespierre and Saint-Just.

First Empire

In 1799, Napoleon Bonaparte became first consul, and later made himself emperor. For Paris, he performed all the functions of an enthusiastic mayor, scarcely hindered by his military expeditions abroad. In Moscow, for instance, he found time to draw up statutes for the Comédie Française. Detailed maps of Paris and architectural plans for new buildings

Guillotine bridge

Masonry from the Bastille was used to build the bridge leading to what was then the place de la Révolution – now place de la Concorde – where the guillotine was erected.

Napoleon Bonaparte

were always part of his baggage. For all his spectacular monuments – the Arc de Triomphe and the column of the Grande-Armée on place Vendôme, for example – the emperor was proudest of his civic improvements: better fresh water supplies, improved drainage, new food markets and a streamlined municipal administration and police force. Most of his reforms survived long after his final defeat in 1815.

The Restoration

Although the monarchy was restored, it faced an ever-present threat in Paris from dissatisfied workers, radical intellectuals and a highly ambitious bourgeoisie. In July 1830 protest turned to riots and the building of barricades; Charles X was forced to abdicate. However, instead of restoring the republic, the revolutionary leaders played it safe and accepted the moderate Louis-Philippe, the so-called 'Citizen King'.

The Revolution of 1848, which brought Louis-Philippe's monarchy to an end, likewise started with riots and barricades in the streets of Paris. A mob threatened the royal palace, forcing the king to flee, and then invaded the Chamber of Deputies, demanding a republic. Elections followed, but they showed that however radical Paris might be, the rest of France was still largely conservative. The new National Assembly withdrew the concessions that had been made to the workers, and up went the barricades again. This time the army was called in with its heavy guns. At least 1,500 insurrectionists were killed, and thousands deported.

Second Empire

The democratically elected president, Louis-Napoleon (a nephew of Napoleon Bonaparte, whose son had died young), seized absolute power in 1851 and the following year became Emperor Napoleon III. Fear led him to modernise Paris. The insurrections of 1830 and 1848 had flared up in the densely populated working-class districts around the centre, and he wanted to prevent a recurrence. He commissioned Baron Georges Haussmann to do away with the narrow alleys that nurtured discontent, and move the occupants to the suburbs. The city was opened up with broad avenues; these so-called *grands boulevards* were too wide for barricades and gave the artillery a clear line of fire in case of revolt.

This Second Empire was a time of joyous abandon and expansion, but the emperor stumbled into war against Prussia in 1870. The army was quickly defeated, and Napoleon III's disgrace and capture brought the proclamation of a new republic, followed by a crippling Prussian siege of Paris. The city held out, albeit reduced to starvation level. When France's leaders agreed to peace, there was another uprising.

Third and Fourth Republics

The Paris Commune (self-rule by the workers) lasted 10 weeks, from 18 March to 29 May 1871, until Adolphe Thiers, the first president of the Third Republic, sent in troops from Versailles to crush it. In the last days, the *communards* set fire to the Palais des Tuileries and executed hostages, including the Archbishop of Paris. The government took revenge: at least 20,000 Commune supporters were killed in the fighting or executed later.

Prosperity rapidly returned, marked by a great construction boom. Projects begun under Napoleon III, such as the Palais-Garnier and the huge Les Halles market, were completed. The city showed off its new face at the 1889 World Fair, with the Eiffel Tower as its monumental centrepiece. The splendid Métro system was inaugurated in 1900.

After this period of peace, however, two wars took their toll. The Germans failed to take Paris during World War I, but occupied it for four years (1940–44) in World War II. The city escaped large-scale bombing, and Hitler's vengeful order to destroy the city before retreating was ignored. Liberation came eventually, with a grand parade down the Champs-Elysées by General Charles de Gaulle, his Free French forces and US and British allies.

General Charles de Gaulle

The post-war city regained its cultural lustre under the influence of figures such as Camus, Sartre, Juliette Gréco and be-bop musicians. Under a rapid succession of governments, however, economic recovery was slow.

Fifth Republic

The Fourth Republic collapsed in 1958 after an army revolt in the colonial war in Algeria. Recalled from retirement, de Gaulle became the first president of the Fifth Republic and set about the task of restoring French prestige and morale.

From the 1968 Riots to Mitterrand's Presidency

Barricades and insurrection hit Paris again in May 1968. With workers on strike, students hurled the Latin Quarter's paving stones at the Establishment. But national elections showed that Paris was once more at odds with most of France, which voted for stability. Succeeding de Gaulle, Georges Pompidou affirmed the new prosperity with controversial riverside expressways and skyscrapers, and the striking Beaubourg cultural centre that bears his name.

In 1977 Jacques Chirac became the first democratically elected mayor of Paris in over a century. At a time when politicians could double as mayor and prime minister, Parisians benefited from leaders who furthered their national political ambitions with a dynamic municipal performance. Although many questioned his taste in the shopping mall that replaced the old markets of Les Halles, Chirac is credited with the effective clean-up of the formerly dirty streets.

President François Mitterrand (1981–95) made his mark on the Paris skyline with a series of imposing works (his *grands projets*): the pyramid centrepiece of the reorganised Louvre, the Grande Arche de La Défense, the Opéra Bastille, the Institut du Monde Arabe and the national library that bears his name.

Family Values

France's birthrate of 1.9 children per family exceeds the European average but is still a source of concern for the state. Every *famille nombreuse* (with three children or more) is rewarded with benefits including nursery provision, subsidised public transport, car tax and school meals, as well as free admission to museums. In 2009 the population of France reached 62.5 million, higher than that of the UK (at 61.6 million). The birthrate has been boosted by France's large Muslim community, whose numbers are, according to many demographers, steadily rising.

Nicolas Sarkozy

Paris Today

Chirac became president in 1995. Within two years, however, his popularity had dwindled, and the socialist leader Lionel Jospin became prime minister. Their period of joint stewardship was one of economic growth, reduced unemployment and rising property values.

In the 2001 mayoral election, the winner was Bertrand Delanoë, the city's first socialist mayor for 130 years. Although Chirac beat National Front candidate Jean-Marie Le Pen in the 2002 presidential election, the huge support for Le Pen shocked the world.

In his second term, President Chirac led a determined opposition to the war in Iraq, which saw his approval ratings at home soar, only to plummet after initiating reforms to the state pension and benefit system. His party's candidate to succeed him, Nicolas Sarkozy, won the presidency in May 2007 with promises of sweeping economic and social reforms. But within months, his high-handed style and fondness for luxury – and whirlwind marriage to former supermodel Carla Bruni – had alienated French voters. Nothing daunted, in 2008 the unpopular Sarkozy announced plans to enact the biggest shake-up of Paris since Haussmann: the so-called 'Grand Paris' scheme that aimed to make the capital and its suburbs a single administrative unit on a par with Greater London. In 2009, teams of international architects delivered their proposals to reshape huge swathes of the city, especially in the east. Sarkozy may be disliked, but he clearly intends to leave his mark on Paris.

Historical Landmarks

c250BC Celtic settlement on island in the River Seine.
52BC Roman conquest, followed by expansion to Left Bank.
508 Clovis, King of Franks, makes Paris his capital.
987 Hugues Capet elected King of France.
1420 The English occupy Paris.
1431 Henry VI of England crowned King of France.
1436 English expelled.
1594 Henri IV enters Paris.
1682 Louis XIV moves court to Versailles.
1789 Storming of Bastille starts French Revolution.
1793 Execution of Louis XVI and Marie-Antoinette; Reign of Terror.
1804 Napoleon Bonaparte becomes emperor.
1814–15 Fall of Napoleon; restoration of Bourbon monarchy.
1830 Bourgeois revolution; Louis-Philippe, the Citizen King.
1848 Revolution brings Louis-Napoleon to power.
1870–1 Franco-Prussian War; Second Empire ends; Paris besieged.
1871 Paris Commune – 10 weeks of workers' rule.
1900 First Métro line opened.
1914–18 World War I. Germans advance to within eight miles of Paris.
1939 World War II begins.
1940 French government capitulates; Germans occupy Paris.
1944 Free French and other Allied forces liberate Paris.
1958 Fall of Fourth Republic. De Gaulle becomes president.
1968 Student riots, workers' general strikes.
1977 Jacques Chirac becomes first elected mayor since 1871.
1981 President Mitterrand elected president.
1995 Jacques Chirac elected president.
2002 The euro replaces the franc as France's unit of currency.
2005 Friction in the Paris suburbs sparks unrest across France.
2007 Nicolas Sarkozy elected president.
2008 Bertrand Delanoë re-elected mayor.
2009 Architects present their plans for the 'Grand Paris' scheme.

WHERE TO GO

Paris is an easy city to navigate. Much of it is easily covered on foot, and it has efficient bus and Métro systems. The biggest divide is between the Rive Droite (Right Bank) and Rive Gauche (Left Bank) on either side of the river Seine, which cuts through the heart of the city. Each Bank has its own connotations: the Right as the business and commercial powerhouse; the Left as the place for intellectuals and learning. There is also an east-west divide between traditionally wealthy western Paris and poorer eastern Paris. But these divisions have their nuances: arty centres of creation are now more likely to be in northeast Paris than affluent, unaffordable St-Germain-des-Prés, and young urban professionals are increasingly buying into the affordable, traditionally working-class districts.

Administratively, the city is divided into 20 *arrondissements*, starting with the 1st in the centre (taking in part of Ile de la Cité and the area around the Louvre) and spiralling outwards clockwise to end at the 20th in the northeast. Confusingly, although Parisians often refer to the *arrondissement* in which they live, they also refer to the historic *quartiers*, such as the Marais, St-Germain, Bastille or Latin Quarter, that in some cases straddle *arrondissements* (the Marais, for example, extends into the 3rd and the 4th *arrondissements*; the Latin Quarter into the 5th and the 6th).

Opposite: soaring Eiffel Tower
Right: Metro sign

Notre-Dame and the eastern end of the Ile de la Cité

ILE DE LA CITÉ

During the 3rd century BC, the Celtic tribe of the Parisii built their first huts on the Ile de la Cité, the largest island in the Seine. In 52BC, Roman legions conquered the settlement and founded Lutetia Parisiorum on the left bank. During the Middle Ages, the island was the centre of political, religious and judicial power, not only for Paris but for the whole of France. Nowadays, the island is still the geographical centre of the capital and home to several of the city's main official buildings. Sainte-Chapelle and Notre-Dame make the island an enduring focus for religious tourism in the city.

Notre-Dame

1 Dominating the island is **Notre-Dame** (daily 8am–6.45pm, tel: 01 42 34 56 10, visits restricted during services, www.notredamedeparis.fr). The cathedral has played a religious

role for at least 2,000 years. In Roman times a temple to Jupiter stood here; in the 4th century AD a Christian church, St-Etienne, was built on the site; this was joined two centuries later by a second church, dedicated to the Virgin. Norman raids left them both in a sorry state, and, in the 12th century, Bishop Maurice de Sully decided that a cathedral should be built to replace them.

The main part of Notre-Dame, begun in 1163, took 167 years to finish. Its transition from Romanesque to Gothic has been called a perfect representation of medieval architecture – an opinion that has provoked some dissent. Cistercian monks protested that such a sumptuous structure was an insult to the godly virtue of poverty, and today many architectural purists still find Notre-Dame excessive.

The original architect is unknown, but Pierre de Montreuil (who was involved in the building of Sainte-Chapelle, *see page 32*) was responsible for much of the 13th-century work. The present look of the cathedral is due to Eugène Viollet-le-Duc, who from 1845 to 1863 restored it to repair the ravages of the 18th century, caused more by pre-Revolutionary meddlers than by revolutionaries who stripped it of religious symbols. Popular support for the expensive restoration was inspired by Victor Hugo's novel *Notre-Dame de Paris*.

The cathedral has witnessed numerous momentous occasions over the centuries, including, in 1239, the procession of Louis IX, during which the pious king walked barefoot, carrying his holy treasure – believed to be Christ's crown of

Notre-Dame's rose window

thorns. In 1594 Henri IV made his politically motivated conversion to Catholicism here to reinforce his hold on the French throne. Napoleon crowned himself emperor at Notre-Dame, upstaging the Pope, who had come to Paris expecting to do it; the scene is depicted in Jacques-Louis David's vast painting, *The Consecration of Napoleon,* now in the Louvre. More recent occasions include General de Gaulle marking the 1944 Liberation of Paris with a Mass here, and in 1970 his death was also commemorated here.

The West Front

Across the three doorways of the west front, the 28 statues of the **Galerie des Rois** represent the kings of Judah. These are 19th-century restorations: the originals were torn down during the Revolution because they were thought to depict kings of France (21 of them were discovered in 1977 and

Notre-Dame's magnificent Gothic west front

moved to the Musée du Moyen Age, *see page 69*).

The central **rose window** depicts the Redemption after the Fall. Two more outsized rose windows illuminate the transept; the northern one retains most of its 13th-century glass. A 14th-century *Virgin and Child* is to the right of the choir entrance.

War memorial

Behind Notre-Dame is the Mémorial des Martyrs de la Déportation, a reminder of the 200,000 French who died in concentration camps during World War II. A dark staircase leads down to a crypt (daily 10am–noon, 2–5pm, until 7pm in summer), where the names of deportees are inscribed on the walls.

The 255-step climb up the **north tower** (daily Apr–Sept 10am–6.30pm, Oct–Mar 10am–5.30pm, www.monuments-nationaux.fr) is rewarded with glorious views of Paris and close-ups of the roof and Notre-Dame's famous gargoyles. Cross over to the south tower – and another 122 steps – to see the 13-ton bell, the only one still remaining (the Revolutionaries melted down the others to make cannons). The bell was re-cast in the 1680s. A further 124 steps lead to the top of the south tower for more spectacular views.

Napoleon III's town planner Baron Haussmann *(see page 21)* greatly enlarged the *parvis*, or cathedral forecourt, diminishing the impact of the towering west front. Excavations beneath the square have revealed walls and foundations from the Gallic, Roman and medieval eras, which now form part of an exhibition on early Paris.

Palais de la Cité

The other architectural and historical highlight on the Ile de la Cité is the **Palais de la Cité**, the complex of buildings that includes the Conciergerie, Sainte-Chapelle and the Palais de Justice, the headquarters of the French supreme court.

The Conciergerie is a museum to its bloody past

Palais de Justice

The imposing neoclassical **Palais de Justice** (Mon–Sat 1.30–6pm, www.ca-paris.justice.fr), heart of the French legal system, stands on the site of the Roman palace where Emperor Julian was crowned in AD360. The lobby (Salle des Pas Perdus) is well worth a visit to catch a glimpse of the lawyers, plaintiffs, witnesses, court reporters and hangers-on.

Conciergerie

Adjacent is the **Conciergerie** (daily Mar–Oct 9.30am–6pm, Nov–Feb 9am–5pm, www.monuments-nationaux.fr), originally the residence of the king's concierge. The 'medieval' facade dates from the 1850s. The building's notoriety, however, dates from the late 18th century: in 1793, at the height of the Terror, the Conciergerie became the antechamber of the guillotine, with around 2,500 prisoners spending their last night here *(see page 19)*. It is now a museum to its bloody past, displaying items including a guillotine blade, the crucifix before which Marie-Antoinette prayed while captive here, and the lock used on Robespierre's cell. Look out on the Cour des Femmes, where husbands, wives and lovers were allowed a final tryst before the tumbrels came to carry off the prisoners.

Sainte-Chapelle

Concealed in the courtyard between the Palais de Justice
2 and the Conciergerie is the magnificent Gothic **Sainte-Chapelle** (daily Mar–Oct 9.30am–6pm, Nov–Feb 9am–

5pm, www.monuments-nationaux.fr). The chapel was constructed in 1248 to designs by Pierre de Montreuil to house holy relics, fragments of which were believed to be Christ's Crown of Thorns, bought by pious King Louis IX (later St-Louis). The lower chapel, with its star-patterned ceiling, was used by palace servants. More impressive is the upper level, where light blazes through 15-m (3¼-ft) high glass windows separated by buttresses so slim that there seems to be no wall at all. Of the 1,134 individual pieces of glass, 720 are 13th-century originals.

Between 1789 and 1815 Sainte-Chapelle served various roles: as a flour warehouse in the Revolution, as a club for high-ranking dandies, then as an archive for Napoleon's Consulate. This latter role fortunately saved the chapel from projected destruction, since the bureaucrats could not think of another site in which to keep their mountains of paper.

Sainte-Chapelle's lower chapel

Other Attractions on the Ile de la Cité

Towards the western end of the island is the pretty, tree-shaded **square du Vert-Galant** and, beyond it, a statue of Henri IV and the recently restored **Pont-Neuf**, which, despite its name – 'New Bridge' – is the oldest bridge in Paris. Its survival is due to the fact that it is made of stone, rather than wood, and also because it was the first bridge in Paris to be constructed without houses on it. In 1985, the Pont-Neuf hit the headlines when Bulgarian-born American artist Christo wrapped the entire structure in fabric.

At the eastern end of the island is the colourful **Marché aux Fleurs** on place Louis Lépine, opposite the Préfecture de Police and Hôtel Dieu. The latter, now a hospital, was built on the site of a medieval hospital; it was the scene of intense battles when the police rose up against the Germans in 1944. In contrast to these forbidding structures, the market is an array of small glasshouses selling flowers and plants. On Sunday, the stalls become a market for caged birds.

ILE ST-LOUIS

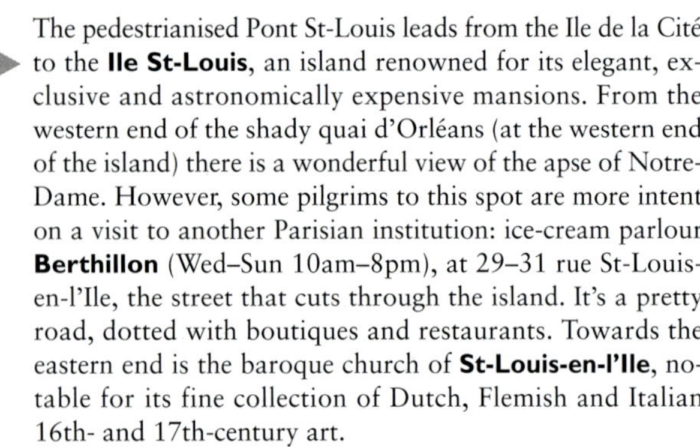

The pedestrianised Pont St-Louis leads from the Ile de la Cité
3 to the **Ile St-Louis**, an island renowned for its elegant, exclusive and astronomically expensive mansions. From the western end of the shady quai d'Orléans (at the western end of the island) there is a wonderful view of the apse of Notre-Dame. However, some pilgrims to this spot are more intent on a visit to another Parisian institution: ice-cream parlour **Berthillon** (Wed–Sun 10am–8pm), at 29–31 rue St-Louis-en-l'Ile, the street that cuts through the island. It's a pretty road, dotted with boutiques and restaurants. Towards the eastern end is the baroque church of **St-Louis-en-l'Ile**, notable for its fine collection of Dutch, Flemish and Italian 16th- and 17th-century art.

The mansions of the Ile St-Louis and beyond

On the northeastern end of the island, at 17 quai d'Anjou, is the grand **Hôtel Lauzun**, built in 1640 by Louis Le Vau, architect to Louis XIV, and now owned by the Rothschild family. It was here that the poets Théophile Gautier and Charles Baudelaire lived in 1845, and where Baudelaire wrote part of *Les Fleurs du Mal*. In the **Hôtel Lambert**, on the corner of rue St-Louis-en-l'Ile, Voltaire enjoyed a tempestuous love affair with the lady of the house, the Marquise du Châtelet.

On the island's south bank is the small **Musée Adam Mickiewicz** (by reservation only Thur 2.15–5.45pm, tel: 01 55 42 83 88). A Polish poet, Mickiewicz (1798–1855) lived in Paris from 1832 to 1840 and devoted himself to helping oppressed Poles. The 17th-century building in which the museum is housed also includes the Polish Library and displays memorabilia of the Polish composer Frédéric Chopin.

Old and new at the Louvre

THE LOUVRE, TUILERIES & CONCORDE

Palais du Louvre

Eight centuries in the making, but with great architectural harmony nonetheless, the **Louvre** was originally built as a fortress by Philippe Auguste in 1190. When Louis XIV moved his court to Versailles, he abandoned the Louvre to artists and other squatters. The Revolutionaries made it a public museum in 1793. As the home of the *Mona Lisa,* the Louvre drew almost unmanageable crowds, until President Mitterrand ordered its re-organisation in the 1980s. A vast new reception area was excavated and topped by the glass **Pyramid** by Sino-American architect I.M. Pei, now the main entrance.

Musée du Louvre

4 The **Musée du Louvre** (Wed–Mon 9am–6pm, Wed and Fri until 10pm, closed public holidays, tickets are valid all day

and allow re-entry into the museum, tel: 01 40 20 50 50, www.louvre.fr) is divided into three wings: Richelieu in the north, Sully in the east and Denon in the south. The collections are arranged in colour-coded sections, to facilitate orientation. An excellent map is available at the ticket desks.

The following is a brief summary of the Louvre's many treasures, including information on the highlights in the different sections.

Lower-Ground and Ground Floors

A good place to start from is the exhibition on the medieval Louvre, on the lower-ground floor of the Sully Wing. This is where the remains of Philippe-Auguste's fort and keep, and some of the artefacts discovered in excavations in the 1980s, can be seen. Above, on the ground floor of the Sully Wing, are Egyptian and Greek Antiquities, and on the ground floor of the Denon wing are Etruscan and Roman antiquities including the *Sarcophagus of a Married Couple* and a *Borghese Gladiator,* and Italian sculpture such as Michelangelo's *Dying Slave* and Canova's neoclassical *Psyche and Cupid* (1793).

Making the Most of the Museums

Entry charges for museums range from around €5–12, with reduced rates for children, students and pensioners. Some museums charge less on Sunday, and entrance is always free on the first Sunday of the month for the following: the Louvre, Musée d'Orsay, Centre Pompidou, Musée de l'Orangerie, Musée Rodin, Musée Picasso and Musée du Moyen Age. The **Paris Museum Pass** (www.parismuseumpass.com) gives entry to over 60 museums and monuments in Paris and its surroundings, including the Louvre and Versailles. You can buy passes valid for two, four or six consecutive days at museums, tourist offices and Métro stations.

The lower ground floor of the Richelieu wing showcases French sculpture, including Guillaume Coustou's giant *Horses of Marly*. On the ground floor of the Richelieu wing, the French sculpture collection continues, with works spanning the 5th to 18th centuries. Also here are Mesopotamian finds such as the black basalt Babylonian *Code of Hammurabi* (1792–1750BC), one of the world's first legal documents.

First Floor

The first floor is where some of the biggest crowd-pullers are housed. On the first floor of the Denon Wing is a spectacular collection of large-format French painting, notably Delacroix's *Liberty Leading the People*, Géricault's *Raft of the Medusa* and David's *Consecration of Napoleon*. Adjacent is a room showcasing Leonardo da Vinci's enigmatic Florentine noblewoman, the *Mona Lisa* (known in French as *La Joconde*). This

Inside the Louvre

iconic piece, painted in 1503, hangs alongside Veronese's vast *Wedding at Cana* and other masterpieces of the Venetian Renaissance.

At the staircase dividing the Denon and Sully wings is the *Winged Victory of Samothrace* (2nd century BC), a Hellenistic figurehead commemorating a victory at sea, and the glittering Galerie d'Apollon (Apollo's Gallery), home to the crown jewels. At this point you reach the Sully Wing and the graceful Hellenic statue of the *Venus de Milo* (2nd century BC), bought by the French government for 6,000 francs in 1820 from the island of Milos. Most of the first floor of the Richelieu Wing houses works of the decorative arts.

Leonardo's *Mona Lisa*

Second Floor

The whole second floor is dedicated to painting, with highlights including Dürer's *Self-Portrait*, Vermeer's *The Lacemaker,* Watteau's *Pierrot* and Ingres's *The Turkish Bath*. The Richelieu Wing houses works from Flanders, the Netherlands, Germany and France (14th to 17th centuries); the second floor of the Sully Wing is devoted to French paintings of the 17th, 18th and 19th centuries.

Additional Museums

In a separate wing are three other collections (entrance at 107 rue de Rivoli, all Tue–Fri 11am–6pm, Sat–Sun 10am–6pm). The **Musee des Arts Décoratifs** presents a survey of interior design, from medieval tapestries to 21st-century design. The **Musée des Arts de la Mode et du Textile** covers Paris fashions and textiles from the 16th century to the present, and, upstairs, the **Musée de la Publicité** is home to a rich collection of posters from the Middle Ages to the present.

Palais-Royal

The **Palais-Royal**, located directly north of the Louvre, across rue de Rivoli, was built in 1639 as Cardinal Richelieu's residence. It gained its regal title when Anne of Austria moved in with young Louis XIV. This serene, arcaded palace has a colourful past. In the days of Philippe d'Orléans, Prince Regent while Louis XV was a child, it was the scene of notorious orgies. A later duke (another Philippe) added apartments above the arcades, along with two theatres (one now the Comédie Française, *see page* 96), shops, gambling houses and fashionable cafés.

Arcades of the Palais-Royal

Despite efforts to curry favour with the revolutionaries, such as calling himself Philippe Egalité (equality), the duke ended up on the guillotine with the rest of the family. After the Revolution, the palace became a gambling den again and narrowly escaped destruction during the 1871 uprising. Following restoration (1872–6), however, it regained respectability.

It now houses the Ministry of Culture, the Council of State, the Constitutional Council, some shops and the historic Grand Véfour restaurant *(see page 108)*.

Cour d'Honneur

In 1986, artist Daniel Buren installed rows of black-and-white-striped stone columns in the Palais-Royal's main quadrangle, the Cour d'Honneur.

Near the Palais-Royal

East of the Palais-Royal is the **Banque de France**, and immediately north is the **Bibliothèque Nationale Richelieu** (National Library, Mon 2–8pm, Tue–Thur 10am–7pm, Sun noon–6pm, tel: 01 53 79 53 79, www.bnf.fr). The latter became a royal library in 1368, when Charles V placed 973 manuscripts in the Louvre. Most of the millions of books, engravings and ancient manuscripts it has accumulated over the centuries have been transferred to the newer national library on the Left Bank *(see page 73)*. The old building with its splendid reading room (1863) has been transformed into a specialist research library.

The Tuileries

West of the Louvre is the one of the city centre's main green spaces, the **Jardin des Tuileries** (daily Mar–Sept 7am–9pm, Oct–Feb 7.30am–7pm), named after a 13th-century tile works and beautifully landscaped according to plans by André Le Nôtre. Walk around the chestnut and lime trees, and admire sculptor Aristide Maillol's sensual statues of nymphs and lan-

Catching some rays in the Tuileries

guorous maidens, a few of which are coquettishly half concealed behind a miniature maze. The gardens' 28 hectares (69 acres) extend across the site of the royal Palais des Tuileries, burnt down during the 1871 Commune *(see page 21)*.

At the eastern entrance to the Tuileries is the pink **Arc de Triomphe du Carrousel**, built at roughly the same time as the Arc de Triomphe *(see page 57)*. The latter is visible from here in a straight line beyond the Obelisk on place de la Concorde. The same axis continues into the distant haze to the skyscrapers of La Défense.

Jeu de Paume and Musée de l'Orangerie

A few fragments of the Palais des Tuileries can be seen by the **Jeu de Paume**, in the northwest corner of the gardens. Once home to real-tennis courts (hence the name) and, later, to the collection of Impressionist paintings now displayed at the Musée d'Orsay *(see page 76)*, the building is currently the attractive showcase for the **Centre National de la Photographie** (Tue noon–9pm, Wed–Fri 12.30–7pm, Sat–Sun 10am–7pm, www.jeudepaume.org). The centre is the showcase for changing exhibitions on all photographic disciplines, including major fashion retrospectives and contemporary video installations.

In the southwestern corner of the Tuileries is the **Musée de l'Orangerie** (Wed–Mon 12.30–7pm, Fri until 9pm, www.musee-orangerie.fr). The building was constructed as a hot-house by Napoleon III, but, since the 1920s, has been the showcase for eight of Claude Monet's water-lily paintings, in which the Impressionist painter captured the play of colour on the pond in his Japanese garden at Giverny *(see page 88)* at different times of day. Extensively renovated and reopened in 2006, the two vast oval rooms upstairs show off the paintings as specified by Monet. In the gallery space downstairs is the Jean Walter and Paul Guillaume Collection, an exceptional array of works by artists including Cézanne, Renoir, Matisse, Picasso, Soutine, Modigliani, Utrillo and Henri Rousseau.

Place de la Concorde

Ange-Jacques Gabriel designed the vast **place de la Concorde** as place Louis XV in 1753, but the Revolutionaries dispensed with all royal connotations. The King's statue was replaced with a guillotine, used to behead Louis XVI and over 1,000 other victims. In 1934, the square was the scene of bloody anti-government rioting by French fascists. 6

In the centre of the square is a pink-granite, 23-m (75-ft) tall Obelisk, a gift from Mohammed Ali, viceroy of Egypt. Dating from 1300BC and once part of the temple of Ramses II in Luxor, it was erected here in 1836.

The two horses guarding the entrance to the Champs-Elysées *(see page 56)* are replicas of the 18th-century *Horses of Marly*, sculpted by Guillaume Coustou (originals in the Louvre, *see page 38*).

Death toll

According to official estimates, 1,119 people were decapitated on place de la Concorde, including Louis XVI, his queen Marie-Antoinette, Charlotte Corday, the poet André Chénier and, ironically, even Revolutionary leader Robespierre.

THE GRANDS BOULEVARDS

North of the Louvre and Tuileries are the Grand Boulevards, a line of wide avenues running from west to east. The boulevards date from the 17th century, when Louis XIV tore down the medieval walls around Paris and created broad, tree-lined spaces. In the 19th century Baron Haussmann extended the string westwards, and the western end of what was named boulevard Haussmann became the preserve of the rich. Today stretches of the central boulevards are dominated by high-street clothing chains, although traces of Second Empire extravagance can still be seen in the ornate balconies and facades.

Palais Garnier

Dominating the place de l'Opéra is the city's historic opera
7 house, the **Palais Garnier** (daily 10am–5pm, guided tours

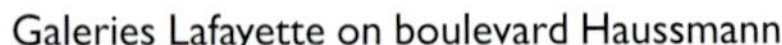

Galeries Lafayette on boulevard Haussmann

in English 11.30am and 2.30pm, July–Aug daily, Sept–June Wed, Sat–Sun, tel: 01 40 01 22 63, www.operadeparis.fr), which puts on opera and ballet in tandem with the newer Opéra Bastille *(see page 54)*.

Chagall ceiling, Palais Garnier

In 1860 architect Charles Garnier was commissioned by Napoleon III to build an opera house, and his lavish designs were in tune with the pomp and opulence that characterised the Second Empire. The five-tiered auditorium, dripping with velvet and gilt, is dominated by a vast chandelier, which crashed down on the audience during a performance in 1896. The auditorium ceiling was painted by Marc Chagall in 1964. Tours also take in the library and museum, showcasing scores, costumes and sets.

Madeleine

A stock exchange, the Bank of France, a theatre: these were among the uses proposed for the huge neoclassical church of **La Madeleine** (daily 9am–7pm), in the centre of place de la Madeleine. Napoleon wanted it as a temple of glory for his army, but his architect suggested the Arc de Triomphe for that use instead. The restored monarchy opted to use the Madeleine as a church, and the building was finally consecrated in 1842. Climb the steps for great views down rue Royale to place de la Concorde and the Assemblée Nationale. 8

Place de la Madeleine is also home to luxury food shops, including Fauchon (nicknamed 'millionaire's supermarket'), chocolatier Hédiard and truffle retailers Maison de la Truffe. Also on the square is the Kiosque-Théâtre Madeleine, where you can buy half-price seats for same-day theatre shows.

Musée Jacquemart-André

Not far from the Madeleine, at 158 boulevard Haussmann,
9 is the **Musée Jacquemart-André** (daily 10am–6pm, www.musee-jacquemart-andre.com). The museum displays art and furniture that once belonged to wealthy collector Edouard André and his wife, erstwhile society portrait painter Néllie Jacquemart. The house is magnificent, and its fine-art collection includes works by Bellini, Boucher, David, Donatello, Uccello, Rembrandt and Titian. The gorgeous café, decorated with chandeliers and antiques, is also worth a visit.

Place Vendôme

Louis XIV wanted this square to be an imposing setting for a monument to him, but, after it was laid out in 1699, only his financiers could afford the rent. Today the Ministry of Justice shares the square with banks, famous jewellers and the Ritz hotel. The statue of Louis XIV was overthrown during the Revolution, and its replacement, the Vendôme column, commemorates the victories of Napoleon, cast from 1,250 Austrian cannons captured at Austerlitz and topped by a statue of the emperor. Like him, it was toppled, in the 1871 Commune *(see page 21)* at the instigation of painter Gustave Courbet, who had to pay to have it re-erected two years later.

Jewellery on place Vendôme

The inside-out Centre Pompidou

BEAUBOURG, LES HALLES & THE MARAIS

Sandwiched between the Louvre and Palais-Royal to the west and the Marais to the east, Beaubourg and Les Halles form one of the city's busiest commercial and cultural centres. The biggest landmark is the Centre Pompidou, Paris's modern art museum. The Marais is an elegant, characterful district, with fine mansions, museums, attractive boutiques, kosher grocers, gay bars and cosy cafés bundled together in a labyrinth of narrow streets.

Châtelet and Hôtel de Ville

Place du Châtelet is a good starting point for exploring the area. Flanked by two theatres (Théâtre de la Ville and Théâtre du Châtelet), the square lies above one of Paris's biggest Métro and RER stations.

Opening out at the eastern end of avenue Victoria is the wide esplanade of the **Hôtel de Ville** (Mon–Sat 10am– 10

7pm), the ornate home of the city council. The neo-Renaissance building, with its magnificent Mansard roof, was rebuilt after the 17th-century town hall was destroyed by fire in the 1871 Commune *(see page 21)*. In medieval times, place de l'Hôtel de Ville was the site of hangings and executions, but today, the pedestrianised square is considerably more alluring, especially in the evening, when the fountains are floodlit.

Centre Pompidou

'That'll get them screaming,' said then-President Georges Pompidou, as he approved the plans for the cultural centre bearing his name, but more popularly known as Beaubourg,
11 after its 13th-century neighbourhood. The **Centre Pompidou** (Wed–Mon 11am–9pm, Thur and for some exhibitions until 11pm, www.centrepompidou.fr) was built by architects

Georges, the swish restaurant on top of the Centre Pompidou

Richard Rogers, Renzo Piano and Gianfranco Franchini, and its inside-out design, dominated by external pipes, tubes, scaffolds and escalators, caused controversy when unveiled in 1977. The pipes are not just for show: the blue ones convey air, the green ones carry water, the yellow ones contain the electrics, and the red ones conduct heating. The building houses a cinema, library, design centre, music 'laboratory' and museum. The plaza outside is a popular rendezvous point and the site of the Stravinsky Fountain, featuring colourful sculptures by Niki de Saint Phalle.

Stravinsky Fountain

One of the world's finest collections of 20th-century art, the **Musée National d'Art Moderne** (National Museum of Modern Art) is housed on the fourth and fifth floors, with the fifth floor home to modern works from 1905 to the 1960s, and the fourth floor covering contemporary work from the 1960s to the present day. Highlights of the modern period include works by Kandinsky, Klee, Klein, Matisse, Picasso and Pollock, and sections on Dadaism, Bauhaus and Surrealism. The contemporary collection includes pieces by Andy Warhol, Verner Panton, Joseph Beuys, Gerhard Richter and Jean Dubuffet. On level six are temporary exhibitions and the fashionable, minimalist – and expensive – Georges restaurant.

Included within the price of the ticket to the Musée National d'Art Moderne is a visit to a reconstruction of sculptor Constantin Brancusi's studio, Atelier Brancusi (Wed–Mon 2–6pm).

Fontaine des Innocents

Les Halles

For centuries this was the site of the capital's main food market (now located out of town, near Orly), but, to widespread regret, the 19th-century iron-and-glass pavilions were demolished in 1971. Gardens, playgrounds and the partly subterranean, much disliked, shopping centre, **Forum des Halles**, have taken their place – but all are soon to be swept away as part of a colossal renovation programme.

Near Les Halles is the Renaissance **Fontaine des Innocents**, once part of a cemetery but now a popular meeting spot. Bars and restaurants line the adjoining rue Berger and the streets leading off it. Away from the gardens and playgrounds, the quarter has its seedy side: drink and drugs, pickpockets and prostitutes. Rue St-Denis, once primarily a red-light district, is now pedestrianised, but still has a number of sex shops.

The church of **St-Eustache** dominates the north side of Les Halles. Built from 1532 to 1637, the main structure is late Gothic with an imposing Renaissance colonnade on its western facade. The church stages free Sunday organ recitals.

The Marais

This district, to the north of the Ile de la Cité and Ile St-Louis, has successfully withstood the onslaught of modern construction. It provides a remarkably intact record of the development of the city, from the reign of Henri IV at the end of the 16th century to the advent of the Revolution. Built on reclaimed marshland, as its name suggests (*marais* means 'swamp'), the **Marais** contains some of Europe's most elegant Renaissance mansions *(hôtels)*, many of which now serve as museums and libraries. In the 1960s, the government designated the area an historical monument, and conservation and restoration took hold. The big change in the last 20 years has been the steady influx of trendy boutiques and gay bars.

Take the Métro to Rambuteau and start at the corner of rue des Archives and rue des Francs-Bourgeois, named after the poor (not bourgeois at all) who were allowed to live here tax-free in the 14th century. The national archives are stored in an 18th-century mansion, the **Hôtel de Soubise** (Mon, Wed–Fri 10am–12.30pm, 2–5.30pm, Sat–Sun 12–5.30pm, www.archivesnationales.culture.gouv.fr). Across a vast, horseshoe-shaped courtyard, you come across the rococo style of Louis XV's time in the apartments of the Prince and Princess of Soubise.

The elegant Hôtel Carnavalet

Marais Museums

The Marais is home to a number of prestigious museums, including, on rue des Francs-Bourgeois, the grand

Musée Carnavalet (Tue–Sun 10am–6pm, www.carnavalet.paris.fr), which charts the history of the city. The museum is housed in the magnificent Hôtel Carnavalet, which was once home to the lady of let-

Le Petit Fer à Cheval, on rue Vieille-du-Temple

ters Madame de Sévigné. The building's present name comes from the distortion of the name of former owner Françoise de Kernevenoy.

The splendid **Musée** 13
National Picasso (Wed–Mon 9.30am–5.30pm, Apr–Sept until 6pm, www.musee-picasso.fr), nearby at 5 rue Thorigny, is set within the restored Hôtel Salé (the name *salé*, meaning 'salty', derives from the salt tax once levied by its former owner). On display are more than 200 paintings, 158 sculptures and hundreds of drawings, engravings, ceramics and models for stage sets and costumes drawn from the artist's personal collection, as well as works by Braque, Matisse, Miró, Degas, Renoir and Rousseau collected by Picasso.

Another Marais museum, housed in the Hôtel Donon at 8 rue Elzévir, is the **Musée Cognacq-Jay** (Tue–Sun 10am–6pm), which contains a splendid collection of 18th-century paintings, furniture and *objets d'art*, bequeathed to the city by the founders of La Samaritaine. This grand old department store (at Châtelet), known for its impressive Art Deco interior, is currently closed for major safety improvements.

Place des Vosges

Rue des Francs-Bourgeois ends at what many agree is the most
 attractive residential square in Paris, **place des Vosges** (originally place Royale). Henri IV had it laid out in 1605 on the site of an old horse-market, the idea being to have 'all the

houses in the same symmetry'. After the wedding festivities of his son Louis XIII, the gardens became the fashionable place in which to promenade, and, later, a spot for aristocratic duels.

The Romantic writer Victor Hugo lived at No. 6, now a **museum** (Tue–Sun 10am–6pm) housing a small collection of his artefacts. It's primarily worth a visit to see the interior of one of the square's grand mansions.

Jewish Quarter

As the Marais has become popular with bar and boutique owners, the Jewish community has retreated to a small pocket centred on narrow Rue des Rosiers, which is lined with kosher delis and falafel stands. Jewish history is told at the **Musée d'Art et d'Histoire du Judaïsme** (Mon–Fri 11am–6pm, Sun 10am–6pm) on rue du Temple. The **synagogue**, with its Art Nouveau facade by Hector Guimard, is at 4 rue Pavée.

Place des Vosges

BASTILLE & EASTERN PARIS

For years a run-down area, Bastille was given a shot in the arm by the construction of a new opera house in the late 20th century. The area south of here, Bercy, has since become a potent symbol of urban regeneration, with a disused 19th-century railway viaduct and dilapidated wine warehouse district brought back to life and now thriving.

Bastille

No trace of the prison stormed in 1789 remains on the cir-
15 cular **place de la Bastille**. Even the column in the centre commemorates a later revolution, that of 1830. The area was largely ignored, until architect Carlos Ott was commissioned to create a new opera house, the **Opéra Bastille** (guided tours, tel: 01 40 01 19 70, www.operadeparis.fr) as one of Mitterrand's *grands projets* (*see page 23*). Cutting-edge artists and designers, notably fashion designer Jean-Paul Gaultier, moved into the area, and now, in streets such as rue de la Couronne, traditional shops alternate with galleries and cool restaurants. North of the Bastille is rue Oberkampf, where there's a concentration of hip bars and boutiques.

The Opéra Bastille

To the south of the Bastille, at 15–121 avenue Daumesnil, is the **Viaduc des Arts**. In the golden age of the railways, the Viaduc de Paris, built in 1859, supported a train line from Bastille to the Bois de Vincennes. However, as the railways declined in the 20th century, the viaduct fell into disrepair. It was saved from demolition and reopened in 1998, with attractive glass-fronted workshops and craft boutiques occupying its arches.

Eastern Paris

In **Bercy**, old stone-walled warehouses and cobbled streets have been given a new lease of life in the shape of Bercy Village, centred on cour St-Emilion, home to boutiques, restaurants and cafés. On the north side of the Parc de Bercy, a repurposed Frank Gehry building became the new home of the Cinémathèque Française *(see page 96)* in 2005, housing a film museum, research centre, repertory cinema, restaurant and film archive.

Also northeast of the Bastille is **Belleville**, home to an attractive park with panoramic views of Paris.

Père Lachaise Cemetery

The Cimetière du Père Lachaise (daily Nov–Mar 8.30am–5.30pm, slightly longer hours Apr–Oct, www.pere-lachaise.com) has seen an estimated 1,350,000 burials since its foundation in 1804. It even served as a battleground in 1871, when the Communards made a last stand here: the Mur des Fédérés in the southeast corner marks the place where many were executed by firing squad. Tombs of the famous include those of painter Ingres, dancer Isadora Duncan and the composers Rossini and Chopin. Writers such as La Fontaine, Molière, Balzac, Proust and Oscar Wilde – honoured with a fine monument by Jacob Epstein – are also buried here. More recent arrivals include singers Edith Piaf and Jim Morrison, and actor Yves Montand.

CHAMPS-ELYSÉES, TROCADÉRO & WEST

The Champs-Elysées were designed by landscape architect André Le Nôtre in 1667 as an extension of the Tuileries *(see page 41)*. Initially the promenade only reached as far as the Rond-Point des Champs-Elysées (ie less than half its current length). Over a hundred years passed before the rest of the avenue, stretching up to the Arc de Triomphe, was completed. Its reputation has ebbed and flowed with the centuries, and it is currently experiencing something of a comeback as one of this city's most prestigious shopping strips.

View of the Champs-Elysées from the Arc de Triomphe

Champs-Elysées

The commercial stretch of the **Champs-Elysées** runs from the Rond-Point to the Arc de Triomphe. The landmark stores are a new four-storey, multi-brand shopping arcade, LE66, at No. 66; Guerlain at No. 68, with its Rococo-style facade and sumptuous interior; the Aladdin's cave of beauty products, Sephora, at No. 70; and Louis Vuitton at No. 101. The majority of the designer shops are concentrated around avenue Montaigne, the southern end of avenue George V and rue du Faubourg St-Honoré. This is fashion land, where prices for the majority are prohibitive. Fashionable bars and restau-

rants have mushroomed in the surrounding streets with new places including Spoon and Food & Wine.

On the southern side of the Champs, between place Clemenceau and the river, is the imposing, glass-domed
17 **Grand Palais** (Wed–Mon 10am–1pm to visitors with advance tickets and 1–8pm to those without reservations, ticket desks shut 30 mins before closing, www.rmn.fr), constructed for the 1900 World Fair. The Grand Palais hosts several major art exhibitions every year; the colossal building also houses the **Palais de la Découverte** (Tue–Sat 9.30am–6pm, Sun and bank hols 10am–7pm, www.palais-decouverte.fr), which includes a hands-on exhibition of the sciences, with a planetarium as centrepiece.

Across avenue Winston Churchill is the **Petit Palais**, which houses the fine-art collection of the Musée des Beaux-Arts de la Ville de Paris (Tue–Sun 10am–6pm, temporary exhibitions until 8pm Thur).

Famous macaroons

Renowned in Paris for generations for its delectable macaroons, Ladurée, a bakery/restaurant at 75 avenue des Champs-Elysées, is always busy and very chic. Don't leave without trying the melt-in-the-mouth macaroons, which come in a multitude of flavours. There's also a branch at 16 rue Royale.

Arc de Triomphe

Officially renamed **place Charles de Gaulle** after the death of the president in 1970, the circular area at the top of the Champs-Elysées is popularly known to Parisians as *l'Etoile* (the star), after the 12 avenues branching out from its centre. It is dominated by one of the most familiar Paris icons, the
Arc de Triomphe (daily 10am–10.30pm, Apr–Sept until 18
11pm, www.monuments-nationaux.fr). The arch is 50m (164ft) high and 45m (148ft) wide. A trip to the top by the stairs (lift for the disabled only) affords excellent views. It is

from here that you can best appreciate the *tour de force* of geometric planning that the avenues represent.

Napoleon I conceived of the Arc de Triomphe as a tribute to his armies, and it bears the names of hundreds of his marshals and generals, and dozens of victories. No defeats are recorded, naturally, although a few of the victories are debatable. Napoleon himself only ever saw a wood-and-canvas model, since the arch was not completed until the 1830s. It rapidly became the focus for state occasions, such as the return of the emperor's remains from St Helena in 1840 and the funeral of Victor Hugo in 1885. When Hitler arrived in Paris as conqueror in 1940, the Arc de Triomphe was the first sight he wanted to see. And at the Liberation, this was the spot where General de Gaulle began his triumphal march down the Champs-Elysées.

Arc de Triomphe

The interior was entirely renovated in 2008, and equipped with new interactive displays telling the monument's history. Under the arch is the grave of the Unknown Soldier, since 1920 the last resting place of a soldier who died in World War I. The eternal flame was lit here in 1923.

Trocadéro

Dominating place du Trocadéro is the **Palais de Chaillot**, built for the Paris World Fair of 1937. The

Palais de Chaillot

imposing Art Deco palace was designed in the shape of an amphitheatre, with its wings following the original outline of the old Trocadéro in graceful symmetry.

The west wing is home to the **Musée de la Marine** (Wed–Mon 10am–6pm, www.musee-marine.fr), which traces the history of the French navy. The east wing houses the **Cité de l'Architecture et du Patrimoine** (Wed–Mon 11am–7pm, Thur until 9pm, www.archi.fr), opened in 2007, combining Paris's old architecture museum with the Institut Français d'Architecture. Both a museum and a professional research centre, it hosts large-scale exhibitions and has a state-of-the-art public audio-visual centre.

On avenue des Nations-Unies is **Cinéaqua** (daily 10am–8pm, www.cineaqua.com), a vast aquarium with cinema, animation studio – and sushi restaurant. 43 tanks contain 10,000 fish, grouped in mini marine ecosystems.

Down avenue du Président Wilson is the vast **Palais de Tokyo**, built as the Electricity Pavilion for the 1937 World Fair. One wing was intended to hold post-1905 fine art from the municipal fine-art collection; the other wing (now the Site de Création Contemporaine) was planned for the national collection of modern art, divided at that time between the Musée du Luxembourg and the Jeu de Paume. The **Musée d'Art Moderne de la Ville de Paris** (Tue–Sun 10am–6pm, www.mam.paris.fr) opened there in 1961. In 1977 the core collection of French and international art was given a new home at the Centre Pompidou *(see page 48)*.

Whereas the emphasis at the Centre Pompidou is on international art, here the focus is on artists who worked in Paris.

In the other wing is the **Site de Création Contemporaine** (Tue–Sun noon–12am, www.palaisdetokyo.com), where a multi-disciplinary programme focuses on young artists through exhibitions, performances and workshops.

Western Paris

West of the Palais de Chaillot, villagey Passy is an upmarket residential area with a couple of busy shopping streets (rue de Passy and rue de l'Assomption). However, it is also home to the atmospheric **Maison de Balzac** (47 rue Raynouard, Tue–Sun 10am–6pm), where the writer penned much of his great opus *La Comédie Humaine*. The house remains furnished as it would have been at the time, with a rich collection of Balzacian manuscripts and memorabilia on show.

Monet's *Impression, Soleil Levant*

Also in the west of Paris is the **Musée Marmottan-Monet** (2 rue Louis-Boilly, daily 10am–6pm, Tue until 9pm, www.marmottan.com), showcase for the art assembled by collector Louis Marmottan (1856–1932). The displays are comprised mostly of Impressionist masterpieces, including works by Monet, Renoir, Manet and Gauguin, but there is also some exceptional First Empire furniture.

The **Musée Nissim de Camondo** (63 rue de Monceau, Wed–Sun 10am–5.30pm), overlooking Parc Monceau, was built by a wealthy Jewish banking family in the style of the Petit Trianon *(see page 87)* at Versailles. The remarkable collection of tapestries, carpets, porcelain, furniture and paintings, all dating from the 18th century, were bequeathed to the state in 1935 by the passionate art collector, Count Moïse de Camondo, in memory of his son, Nissim, killed in action in 1917. The building and family history are as fascinating as the collection.

Also beside Parc Monceau is the **Musée Cernuschi** (7 avenue Vélasquez, Tue–Sun 10am–6pm), one of the most important collections of Oriental art in Europe. The 19th-century financier Henri Cernuschi amassed the collection on a tour of China and Japan, and built this mansion to house it.

Bois de Boulogne

In western Paris is the capital's biggest park, comprising 900 hectares (2,200 acres) of grassland, lakes and woods. There are bikes for rent outside its entrance. Napoleon III commissioned Baron Haussmann to transform a remnant of an old hunting forest along the lines of a London park, and the **Bagatelle**, once a royal retreat, is the site of a lovely English garden. Also within the park is a craft museum, a boating lake, the **Jardin d'Acclimatation** (an amusement park with attractions for children) and two racecourses: Longchamp for flat races; Auteuil for steeplechases. However, parts of the park after dark are considered to be among the most dangerous places in Paris.

MONTMARTRE & PIGALLE

With narrow, winding streets and dead-ends **Montmartre** (*'la Butte'*, or the hill, to its residents) still has something of a provincial feel. For over 200 years it has been associated with artists and bohemians. The tourist *Montmartrobus* spares you the walk and shows you some of the area in a single sweep, but the best way to discover Montmartre at your own pace is to start early, at the top. Take the Métro to Abbesses and the lift to the street (the stairs here seem endless) – and note the handsome Art Nouveau entrance as you leave. Rue Yvonne le Tac leads to the base station of a funicular railway.

Sacré-Coeur

Sacré-Cœur

The funicular (Métro/bus tickets are valid) climbs to the terrace right in front of the Byzantine-style basilica of **Sacré-Cœur** (basilica daily 6am–10.30pm, crypt and dome 10am–5.45pm, until 6.45pm in summer). Standing at the highest point in Paris, it is one of the city's principal landmarks, and one of the few to remain controversial. Some people still scorn it as a vulgar pastiche, and the working-class residents of the area resented it being erected as a symbol of penitence for the insurrection of the 1871 Commune *(see page 21)* – they did not feel in

the least penitent. The Sacré-Cœur's whiteness comes from the local Château-Landon limestone, which bleaches on contact with carbon dioxide in the air and hardens with age. For many, the best reason to visit the basilica is the view of the city from the dome or the terrace below.

Last vineyard

At the corner of rue St-Vincent and rue des Saules, look out for the city's last surviving vineyard, the tiny Clos de Montmartre, which produces a wine that reputedly 'makes you jump like a goat'.

Place du Tertre

A few steps west of Sacré-Cœur is **St-Pierre-de-Montmartre**, one of the city's oldest churches. Consecrated in 1147, it is a significant work of early Gothic style, belied by its 18th-century facade. Nearby **place du Tertre** was once the centre of village life. The square is best visited early in the morning, before the pushy portrait artists set up their easels and the crowds of tourists take over.

On place Emile Goudeau, just downhill but artistically on an altogether much higher level, No. 13 was the site of the studio known as the **Bateau-Lavoir** (so-called because the building resembled the Seine's laundry boats until it was destroyed by fire). It was here that Picasso, Georges Braque and Juan Gris developed Cubism, Modigliani painted, and Apollinaire wrote his first Surrealist verses. Some of their predecessors – Renoir, Van Gogh and Gauguin – once lived and worked just north of place du Tertre.

The **Cimetière de Montmartre** (daily 8am–5.30pm, slightly longer hours Sun and Apr–Oct) is at 20 avenue Rachel. The cemetery's more illustrious tenants include 19th-century society beauty Madame Récamier, composers Berlioz and Offenbach, the sculptor Degas, German poet Heinrich Heine and film director François Truffaut.

Pigalle

At the far end of rue Lepic, a market street renowned for its
food shops and several appealingly bohemian cafés, is place
Blanche, where the ambience changes. On the corner of
22 boulevard de Clichy is the iconic **Moulin Rouge**, still stag-
ing its nightly cabarets, although mostly to tourists. Next
door is **La Loco**, a huge disco, pumping with the sounds of
house, dance music and mainstream pop. Less artistic attractions abound in **Pigalle**, a powerhouse of the Paris sex
trade for decades. Tassled curtains provide glimpses of smoky
interiors, garish signs promote live sex shows and pushy
bouncers attempt to entice passers-by. However, Pigalle's
sleaze has, in recent years, been tempered by fashionable
nightlife venues. The cabarets which formerly occupied half
the houses along rue des Martyrs are increasingly being taken
over by hip clubs and trendy bars.

Moulin Rouge

LA VILLETTE

La Géode

In northeast Paris, right against the Périphérique ring road, is the **Parc de la Villette** (Métro: Porte de Pantin or Porte de la Villette, daily 6am–1am, www.villette.com). Laid out on the site of an enormous abattoir, which was rendered obsolete by improved refrigeration techniques and poor design (the cows could not get up the steps), 55 hectares (136 acres) of futuristic gardens surround a colossal science museum, the **Cité des Sciences et de l'Industrie** (Tue–Sat 10am–6pm, Sun 10am–7pm, www.cite-sciences.fr). It is not a museum for academics: the exhibits are interactive, with buttons, keyboards and screens to keep mind and body alert.

Begin at 'L'Univers' (Universe), which has a spectacular planetarium and also provides an explanation of the Big Bang. 'La Vie' (Life) is an eclectic mix of medicine, agriculture and economics. 'La Matière' (Matter) reproduces a nuclear explosion and gives you the chance to land an Airbus 320, and 'La Communication' has displays of artificial intelligence, three-dimensional graphics and virtual reality.

La Géode (daily 10.30am–6.30pm, Sat until 9.30pm, Sun until 8.30pm, reservations advised during school holidays and on weekend afternoons, tel: 08 92 68 45 40, lines open noon–8pm, www.lageode.fr) is a giant silver ball housing a wraparound IMAX cinema; see the website for details of the programme. Near here are L'Argonaute, a retired naval submarine, and Cinaxe, a flight-simulator-cum-cinema that's definitely not for the queasy.

The former cattle market now houses a cultural and conference centre in the immense 19th-century Grande Halle, which reopened in 2007 after restoration. Next door, the **Cité de la Musique** is an edifice of angles designed by architect Christian de Portzamparc, and includes the **Musée de la Musique** (Tue–Sat noon–6pm, Sun 10am–6pm, ticket desks close 45 mins prior to last entry, www.cite-musique.fr). Portzamparc also designed the national music and dance conservatory on the other side of the Grande Halle. The museum charts the development of classical, jazz and folk music and houses an impressive collection of over 4,500 musical instruments.

The gardens of the park are the biggest to be built in Paris since Haussmann's time. Designed by Bernard Tschumi and opened in 1993, they comprise several thematic areas such as the Jardin des Frayeurs Enfantines (Garden of Childhood Fears) with a huge dragon slide, and the Jardin des Vents (Garden of Winds), home to multicoloured bamboo. Abstraction continues in the form of Tschumi's folies: red angular 'tree houses' (minus the trees), each with a special function such as play area, workshop, daycare centre or café.

Along the Canal

The Paris canals were dug in 1821 as a transport link for the factories and warehouses in the area northeast of the Bastille. Shielded by trees, the canal is a popular strolling ground, particularly on balmy summer evenings. A pleasant way to experience it is by canal boat, starting either at Bastille or at La Villette. Sights en route include, at the bend in the canal, the trendy Chez Prune café and a row of pastel-coloured Antoine et Lili shopfronts, and on the opposite bank, the Hôtel du Nord, of French movie fame. Canal tours lasting around two and a half hours are run by Canauxrama. Tel: 01 42 39 15 00 or visit www.canauxrama.com for further details.

St-Germain-des-Prés still trades on its literary heyday

LATIN QUARTER & ST-GERMAIN-DES-PRÉS

The area referred to as the Latin Quarter lies to the east of boulevard St-Michel. This maze of ancient streets and squares has been the stamping ground of students for nearly eight centuries, and Latin was virtually the mother tongue until Napoleon put a stop to it after the Revolution. West of boulevard St-Michel is St-Germain-des-Prés, once the centre of literary Paris and existentialism, with the oldest church in Paris at its heart. Although these two areas have changed over the past few decades, with high fashion increasingly replacing heavy thinking, they still maintain their charm in tree-lined boulevards, narrow streets and manicured gardens.

The Latin Quarter

Begin your visit to the Latin Quarter at **place St-Michel**, where students buy their books or gather around the grand

Books are big business

1860s fountain by Gabriel Davioud. From here, plunge into the narrow streets of the **St-Séverin** quarter to the east (rues St-Séverin, de la Harpe and Galande). Here, you'll find medieval streets busy with Greek restaurants, Tunisian bakeries selling sticky date pastries, and art-house cinemas.

The early Gothic church of **St-Julien-le-Pauvre**, on the street of the same name, hosts recitals of chamber and religious music. Just across rue St-Jacques stands the exquisite 13th- to 15th-century flamboyant Gothic church of **St-Séverin**, in which Dante is said to have prayed and Saint-Saëns asked to be made honorary organist.

The Sorbonne

Named after the 13th-century college established by Robert de Sorbon for poor theological students, the university was later taken in hand by Cardinal Richelieu, who financed its reconstruction (1624–42). Few of the somewhat forbidding buildings are open to the public, but you can go inside the 17th-century **courtyard** with its ornate sundial and see the outside of the baroque library and domed church.

Protests against overcrowding, antiquated teaching, bureaucracy and the basis of the social system made the Sorbonne a focal point for unrest in 1968, a year of ferment across Europe. Over on the tree-shaded **place de la Sorbonne**, it's hard to imagine the police invading such a peaceful sanctuary – one that for centuries guaranteed student immunity. But invade they did, and revolt exploded onto the streets. Students and workers made common cause, and there followed widespread national strikes that threatened the survival of the government. In the aftermath of the revolts, the Sorbonne was absorbed into the huge Paris Universities monolith and lost its independence.

Musée National du Moyen Age – Thermes de Cluny

Opposite the Sorbonne's rue des Ecoles entrance is the **Musée National du Moyen Age** (6 place Paul-Painlevé, Wed–Mon 9.15am–5.45pm, www.musee-moyenage.fr), still often called by its former name, the Musée de Cluny. Once the residence of the Abbots of Cluny, the museum houses one of the world's finest collections of medieval artefacts. Its star attraction is the exquisite, 15th-century tapestry *La Dame à la Licorne* (The Lady and the Unicorn), six pieces depicting the five senses and the temptations that the eponymous lady vows to overcome. The museum also holds 21 of the original heads of the Kings of Judah, sculpted in 1220 for Notre-Dame cathedral but vandalised in the Revolution. 23

The Hôtel de Cluny was built on the remains of a huge Gallo-Roman bath house believed to have been erected in AD200 by the guild of *nautes* (boatmen) – ships' prows are carved on the arch supports of the frigidarium (cold bath house).

Musée National du Moyen Age

Great thinkers

Among those interred in the Panthéon are novelist Emile Zola, socialist Jean Jaurès, Louis Braille and Pierre and Marie Curie (the latter was the first woman buried here).

Panthéon

Designed for Louis XV in 1755 as the church of Ste-Geneviève (patron saint of Paris), the neoclassical **Panthéon** (daily 10am–6pm, until 6.30pm in summer) was requisitioned in the Revolution to serve as a mausoleum. For most of the 19th century its status oscillated between secular and sacred, but Victor Hugo's funeral in 1885 settled the issue in favour of a secular mausoleum. The interior is sparse, with its walls covered by 19th-century murals by Puvis de Chavannes. The crypt is a maze of corridors lined with cells containing tombs. 24

Rue Mouffetard

The old streets behind the Panthéon, where the bustling **rue Mouffetard** and its offshoots meet are like a small town within the city. The stalls of rue Mouffetard's morning market are piled with appetising produce. Here, and on tiny **place de la Contrescarpe** nearby, you will find a large choice of ethnic restaurants. A little to the east, signs to **Arènes de Lutèce** point to a little park that is the site of a Roman amphitheatre, partially restored after its remains were found in the 19th century.

In rue St-Etienne-du-Mont is the church of **St-Etienne-du-Mont** (Mon 2.30–7.30pm, Tue–Sun 10am–7pm). This was the parish church of the Abbey of Ste-Geneviève and still houses a shrine to the city's patron saint. The highlight is the Renaissance rood screen (1541), the only one in Paris.

Institut du Monde Arabe

Back by the Seine, but heading east, stroll past the university complex that stands on the site of the former Halles aux Vins (wine market). Designed by architect Jean Nouvel, the nearby **Institut du Monde Arabe** (1 rue des Fossés- 25
St-Bernard, Tue–Sun 10am–6pm, www.imarabe.org) was built with the help of 16 Arab nations to foster cultural links between Europe and the Islamic world. Inside, a museum traces the cultures of the Arab world with first-rate exhibits. A library of over 40,000 volumes covers all aspects of Arab culture. There are fine views from the rooftop restaurant.

Institut du Monde Arabe

Jardin des Plantes

Adjacent is the **Jardin des Plantes** (daily 8am–dusk, until 7.30pm in summer), created by Louis XIII as 'a royal garden of medicinal plants' and still a fine botanical and decorative garden, with exotic plants in the hothouses. The oldest tree in Paris is located here.

The adjoining **Muséum National d'Histoire Naturelle** (Wed–Mon 10am–6pm, www.mnhn.fr) has renovated its venerable exhibits of fossils, skeletons, butterflies and mineral samples. The **Grande Galerie de l'Evolution** (36 rue Geoffroy-St-Hilaire, opening times as above), devoted to the origins of life on earth, is outstanding.

St-Germain-des-Prés

Once the heart of literary Paris, **St-Germain-des-Prés** covers an area stretching roughly from St-Sulpice to the Seine and bounded to the west by boulevard St-Germain. Its elegant streets house chic boutiques, yet it still retains a sense of animation, with crowded cafés spilling out on to the pavements. In the 1950s the area became a breeding ground for literature and philosophy. Writers such as Jean-Paul Sartre, Simone de Beauvoir and Albert Camus, gathered at **Les Deux Magots**, **Café Flore** and other venues.

Boulevard St-Germain

That said, the days of black polo-necks and beret-clad existentialists engaged in heated debate are over. The area has been colonised by designers and upmarket antiques dealers. The Marché St-Germain shows just how much it has changed. After a tasteful restoration, the old market hall now contains fashion boutiques, a swimming pool, an auditorium and small food market.

On the opposite side of the boulevard, the church of **St-Ger- 26
main-des-Prés** (Mon–Sat 8am–7.45pm, Sun 9am–8pm) is the oldest in Paris, parts of it dating from the 11th century. It is named after a former cardinal of Paris, who is buried here.

Académie Française

The august Palais de l'Institut de France, home of the **Académie Française**, is north of the church of St-Germain, on quai de Conti by the Pont des Arts. It was designed by Louis le Vau in 1668 to harmonise with the Louvre across the river. The Institut began as a school for the sons of provincial gentry, financed by a legacy from Cardinal Mazarin. Then, in 1805, the building was turned over to the Institut, which comprises the Académie Française, supreme arbiter of the French language founded by Cardinal Richelieu in 1635, and the Académies des Belles-Lettres, Sciences, Beaux-Arts, and Sciences Morales et Politiques.

New Left Bank

The 'new' Rive Gauche (Left Bank) is the biggest urban renewal project since the mid-1850s. Newly created streets and buildings are going up in a zone of rusty factories and disused railway tracks that extend south along the river from the Gare d'Austerlitz. The area's centrepiece is the controversial **Bibliothèque Nationale de France François Mitterrand** (Mon 2–7pm, Tue–Sat 9am–7pm, Sun 1–7pm, www.bnf.fr), which opened in 1996; its 90-m (300-ft) high glass towers evoke open books. The area's newest addition is the **Cité de la Mode et du Design** at 28 quai d'Austerlitz, which opened in 2009. Its eye-catching bright green riverfront facade has been fixed on a disused warehouse that is home to design shows, restaurants and a performance venue.

Musée Delacroix and St-Sulpice

Tucked away in a tiny square a short walk from the church of St-Germain-des-Prés is the delightful **Musée National Eugène Delacroix** (6 place Furstenberg, Wed–Mon 9.30am–5pm, until 5.30pm in summer, www.musee-delacroix.fr). The painter lived here from 1857 to 1863 while he was working on frescoes in a chapel at St-Sulpice. Temporary exhibitions are held in the airy former studio, and letters and personal effects are displayed in the house. There's a wonderfully calm garden out the back.

A short hop south across boulevard St-Germain-des-Prés is place St-Sulpice, the eastern side of which is dominated by Jean-Baptiste Servandoni's Italianesque church of the same name. **St-Sulpice** (daily 7.30am–7.30pm, www.paroisse-saint-sulpice-paris.org) is notable for its vast towers (under restoration), one of which is higher than the other, and for Delacroix's massive oil-and-wax frescoes, completed two years before his death.

Leisurely pursuits in the Jardin du Luxembourg

Jardin du Luxembourg

The beautifully landscaped **Jardin du Luxembourg** is the 27 quintessential Paris park. Students read, relax or play tennis, old men meet under the chestnut trees to play chess or a game of *boules*, lovers huddle together on metal chairs, and children sail boats across the carp-filled pond and ride a merry-go-round designed by Charles Garnier, architect of the historic opera house *(see page 45)*. At the northern end of the gardens, the Italianate **Palais du Luxembourg** (guided tours by appointment, tel: 01 44 54 19 49 for individuals, www.senat.fr), built for Marie de Médicis in the early 17th century, now houses the French Senate. The adjacent Petit Luxembourg is the official home of the president of the Senate.

The **Musée National du Luxembourg** (19 rue de Vaugirard, Mon, Fri, Sat 10.30am–10pm, Tue, Thur 10.30am–7pm, Sun 9.30am–7pm, www.museeduluxembourg.fr) hosts art exhibitions.

Odéon

The Odéon district lies between the Latin Quarter and St-Germain-des-Prés. Across boulevard St-Germain, at the Carrefour de l'Odéon, a statue of the Revolutionary leader Georges Danton marks the spot where his house once stood. Fellow Revolutionary Camille Desmoulins lived at No. 2 before storming the Bastille in 1789. Others plotted to the north in neighbouring streets that now shelter some of the most expensive boutiques and apartments in Paris.

From here, rue de l'Odéon, the first street in Paris to have gutters and pavements, leads to place de l'Odéon. The neoclassical Odéon Théâtre de l'Europe (tel: 01 44 85 40 40, www.theatre-odeon.fr), founded in 1782, is home to one of France's leading state theatre companies. It puts on a repertoire of mainly foreign playwrights (Büchner, Chekhov, Shakespeare, etc), sometimes in original-language productions.

The old station clock presides over the Musée d'Orsay

AROUND THE EIFFEL TOWER

When the Paris nobility moved out of the Marais *(see page 50)* in the 18th century, and Versailles dwindled, the rich and famous built new town houses across the river from the Tuileries, in the 7th *arrondissement*. Not only is this chic district rich with upmarket architecture, it is also has a wealth of visitor attractions, with highlights including the Musée d'Orsay, the Eiffel Tower, the Invalides and the Musée Rodin.

Musée d'Orsay

'The station is superb and truly looks like a Fine Arts Museum, and since the Fine Arts Museum resembles a station, I suggest... we make the change while we still can,' said painter Edouard Detaille in 1900. In 1986, his joke became a reality. Linked to the Tuileries by the Passerelle Solférino footbridge, the converted 19th-century hotel-cum-railway station was

28 transformed into the **Musée d'Orsay** (Tue–Sun 9.30am–6pm, Thur until 9.45pm, www.musee-orsay.fr), devoted to French art from 1848 to 1914. Keeping the exterior much as it was, Italian architect Gae Aulenti adapted the interior to house many of the previously scattered works of that period, including the superb Impressionist collection formerly held in the Jeu de Paume *(see page 42)*. Sculpture is well represented, and photography is covered from its inception (1839) onwards.

Many visitors start at the top with the Impressionists and Post-Impressionists: Renoir, Cézanne, Manet, Monet, Toulouse-Lautrec, Degas and Van Gogh (this is the best collection of his work outside Amsterdam, with several works from the frenzied months of activity before he died in 1890). Outstanding in the ground-floor collections are the vast canvases of Gustave Courbet. There is a café high up behind the huge old station clock, and on the middle level is the station hotel's beautifully restored restaurant.

Assemblée Nationale

Geographically if not temperamentally part of the Left Bank, the Palais Bourbon is the seat of the **Assemblée Nationale** (33 bis quai d'Orsay), the Lower House of the French Parliament. Built from 1722 to 1728 for Louis XIV's daughter the Duchess of Bourbon, in the style of the Grand Trianon at Versailles, it forms a fittingly stately riverside facade for the grand 7th *arrondissement*. Napoleon added the Grecian columns facing the Pont de la Concorde, but the palace

Sculpture at the Palais Bourbon

is more graceful when seen from its entrance on the south side. Only French citizens can go in, apart from the annual Journées du Patrimoine open days, when thousands queue to see the Delacroix paintings in the library.

Musée Rodin

The Prime Minister's residence, Hôtel Matignon (57 rue de Varenne), is a short walk from the Assemblée Nationale. Its private park has a music pavilion favoured for secret strategy sessions. On the same elegant street, at No. 77, Rodin's former mansion, the delightful 18th-century Hôtel Biron, is now a showcase for the sculptor's works in the form of the **Musée National** 29
Rodin (Tue–Sun, Apr–Sept museum 9.30am–5.45pm, gardens until 6.45pm, last admission at 5.15pm, Oct–Mar museum 9.30am–4.45pm, gardens until 5pm, last admission at 4.15pm, www.musee-rodin.fr). Many of the most famous sculptures are in the gardens. Highlights include *The Kiss* (removed from the Chicago World Fair of 1893 for being too shocking), *The Thinker* (reputedly Dante contemplating the Inferno), *The Burghers of Calais* and *Balzac*, depicting the writer as a mountain of a man. Also on display are works by Camille Claudel, the most famous of Rodin's mistresses.

Rodin's *The Thinker*

Les Invalides

Gilded dome of the Invalides

One of the most important sights in this area is the
30 monumental **Hôtel des Invalides** (daily 10am–5pm, Apr–Sept until 6pm, www.invalides.org), established by Louis XIV as the first national hospital and retirement home for soldiers wounded in action. At one time it housed approximately 6,000 veterans, but Napoleon Bonaparte commandeered a large part of the building for the superb **Musée de l'Armée** (opening times as above), a vast collection of weapons and military paraphernalia dating from medieval times to the modern era. It is, in effect, several museums in one: there are large sections devoted to the two world wars, another to dozens of wonderfully intricate 18th-century models of French towns and fortresses, another to awe-inspiring suits of armour, and a new section to uniforms in 2009.

The Invalides came to symbolise the glory of Napoleon himself, when his remains were brought back from St Helena in 1840 for burial in the chapel under the golden **Dôme** (opening times as above, until 7pm 15 June–15 Sept). The emperor's son, who died of tuberculosis in Vienna, is buried in the crypt; his remains were sent here by Hitler in 1940.

The main courtyard allows access to the adjoining church of **St-Louis-des-Invalides**, decorated with flags taken by French armies in battle. The courtyard itself contains the 18 cannons, including eight taken from Vienna, that Napoleon ordered to

La Pagode

The area around Les Invalides is well worth exploring: start with Paris's quirkiest cinema and tea house, La Pagode in rue de Babylone. The tea is strong, the garden tropical, and the films right up-to-date.

be fired on great occasions, including the birth of his son in 1811. The cannons sounded again for the 1918 Armistice and the funeral of Marshal Foch in 1929.

Southwest of the Invalides is the **Ecole Militaire**, where officers have trained since the middle of the 18th century. Their former parade ground, the vast **Champ de Mars**, is now a green park stretching all the way to the Eiffel Tower.

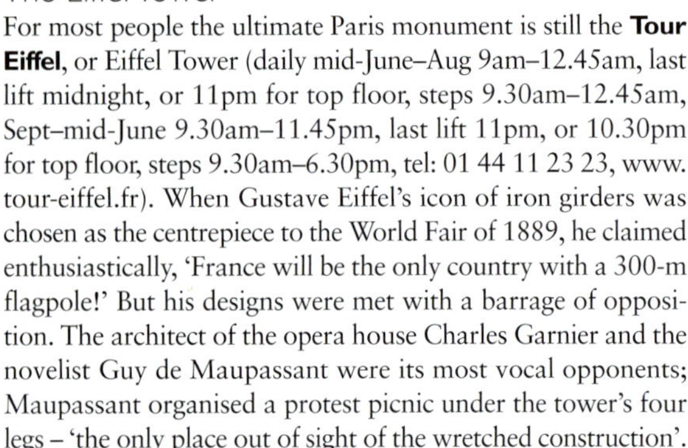

The Eiffel Tower

31 For most people the ultimate Paris monument is still the **Tour Eiffel**, or Eiffel Tower (daily mid-June–Aug 9am–12.45am, last lift midnight, or 11pm for top floor, steps 9.30am–12.45am, Sept–mid-June 9.30am–11.45pm, last lift 11pm, or 10.30pm for top floor, steps 9.30am–6.30pm, tel: 01 44 11 23 23, www.tour-eiffel.fr). When Gustave Eiffel's icon of iron girders was chosen as the centrepiece to the World Fair of 1889, he claimed enthusiastically, 'France will be the only country with a 300-m flagpole!' But his designs were met with a barrage of opposition. The architect of the opera house Charles Garnier and the novelist Guy de Maupassant were its most vocal opponents; Maupassant organised a protest picnic under the tower's four legs – 'the only place out of sight of the wretched construction'.

However, the Paris public loved their new tower, and only a few years later it was being lauded by writers and artists such as Apollinaire, Jean Cocteau, Raoul Dufy and Maurice Utrillo. At 321m (1,054ft) the tower was the world's tallest building until 1931, when New York's Empire State Building was constructed. Surviving a proposal for its demolition in 1909, when the placing of a radio transmitter at the top gave it a valuable practical function, the tower is now climbed by some six million visitors a year.

There are 360 steps to the first level, where there is an audio-visual presentation on the tower's history, and another 700 to the second; both of these floors are also accessible by lifts – there is always a queue for these, which travel 100,000km (62,137 miles) a year. On the third level (accessible by lift only) is a glassed-in viewing platform and Gustave Eiffel's sitting room. On a clear day panoramas of over 65km (40 miles) can be enjoyed. There are two restaurants, including the Michelin-starred Jules Verne *(see page 115)* on the second floor. On hot days the ironwork expands, enabling the tower to grow as much as 15cm (6in). Even in the strongest of winds, it has never swayed more than 12cm (4in). Up to 40 tonnes of paint have to be used when it is painted every seven years.

The Eiffel Tower

Musée du Quai Branly

Just northeast of the tower, at 37 quai Branly, is Jacques Chirac's cultural legacy, the **Musée du Quai Branly** (Tue–Sun 11am–7pm, Thur–Sat until 9pm, www.quaibranly.fr), opened in 2006. The museum houses a collection of around 300,000 objects of art from Africa, Asia, the Americas and Oceania, with over 3,600 items actually on display. With its colonial overtones, the collection has sparked some controversy, but the building itself – a striking foliage-covered scarlet edifice designed by architect Jean Nouvel – has been more warmly received.

MONTPARNASSE

Named after the mountain home of the classical Muses, 'Mount Parnassus' was a mound left after quarrying. In the

A colourful mural in Montparnasse

1920s, the quarter took over from Montmartre as the stamping ground of the city's artistic colony, led by Picasso. American expatriates such as Ernest Hemingway, Gertrude Stein, F. Scott Fitzgerald and John Dos Passos liked the free-living atmosphere and added to the mystique themselves.

The catacombs

Beneath Montparnasse are the city's catacombs (entrance on place Denfert-Rochereau, Tue–Sun 10am–5pm), old quarries whose corridors were used for the reburial of millions of skeletons from overcrowded cemeteries and charnel houses. Unidentified, the bones are stacked on shelves and sometimes artfully arranged into macabre patterns.

One of Henry Miller's hang-outs, Le Select (99 boulevard du Montparnasse) opened as an all-night bar in 1925. *Les Six*, the group of composers that included Milhaud, Poulenc and Honegger, met here. La Coupole *(see page 115)*, opposite at No. 102, was a favourite with Sartre and de Beauvoir in the years after World War II; it has been rebuilt and now seats 400 people. Le Dôme at No. 108 has lost some of its character since the days of Modigliani and Stravinsky, with elaborate remodelling. Across the street, at No. 105, Picasso, Derain and Vlaminck used to meet at La Rotonde. At the junction of boulevard du Montparnasse and boulevard St-Michel, La Closerie des Lilas is where Lenin and Trotsky dreamt of a Russian Revolution, and where Hemingway and his friends met after World War I.

Today the attraction isn't immediately evident: boulevard du Montparnasse is plain by Paris standards, and most of the haunts where the 'Lost Generation' found itself have been polished and painted, or even entirely rebuilt. But people still pay elevated prices for the privilege of sitting in a seat that may have been warmed by Modigliani, Lenin or Sartre.

The 59-storey, 210-m (689-ft) **Tour Montparnasse** (33 avenue du Maine, Apr–Sept daily 9.30am–11.30pm, Oct–Mar Sun–Thur 9.30am–10.30pm, Fri–Sat 9.30am–11pm, last lift half an hour before closing, www.tourmontparnasse56.com) may be something of an egregious eyesore, but the view from the top is marvellous. 33

The **Cimetière du Montparnasse** (entrance on boulevard Edgar Quinet, Mar–Nov 8am–6pm, Sat from 9am, slightly shorter hours in winter) contains the tombs of composers Saint-Saëns and César Franck, writer Maupassant and poet Baudelaire, plus Alfred Dreyfus, the Jewish army officer whose conviction on trumped-up spying charges split the nation. Also buried here are car maker André Citroën, Vichy prime minister Pierre Laval (executed while dying from a suicide attempt) and philosopher Jean-Paul Sartre and his writer companion Simone de Beauvoir.

LA DÉFENSE

Follow the long avenue de la Grande-Armée down from the Arc de Triomphe, and the battery of towers looms larger and larger beyond the elegant, leafy suburb of Neuilly. Cross the river and you are in a mini-Manhattan that has grown since 1969 to become a mini-city in its own right.

 The **Grande Arche** (daily 10am–7pm, Apr–Aug until 8pm, www.grandearche.com) is further away than most of the towers, and only when you get close do you realise how big it is. A hollow cube 110m (360ft) high and 106m (347ft) wide, it could straddle the Champs-Elysées and tuck Notre-Dame underneath it. Built with remarkable speed (Danish architect Johann-Otto von Sprekelsen won the contest in 1983 and the arch was completed in time for the bicentennial of the French Revolution in 1989), the Grande Arche stands in line with the Arc de Triomphe and the Louvre. Its white

gables are clad in Carrara marble, the outer facades with a combination of grey marble and glass. The two 'legs' contain offices, and the roof houses conference rooms and exhibition spaces. A bubble lift whisks you up through a fibreglass and Teflon 'cloud', held by steel cables. At the top is a new museum of computing, which opened in 2008, and a terrace with a panoramic view.

Increasing numbers of visitors and office-workers have given rise to a growing number of shops, cinemas, hotels and restaurants at La Défense. One of the biggest new arrivals is the 16-screen UGC Ciné Cité La Défense cinema complex.

Across the main concourse a 12-m (39-ft) bronze thumb by César literally sticks out like a sore thumb. Stroll down the tiers of terraces and you will discover even more statues, fountains and murals by Miró, Calder and other modern artists, all detailed on street-plans given out at information desks.

The Grande Arche at La Défense

The view of Versailles from the gardens

EXCURSIONS

Versailles

35 Louis XIV's palace at **Versailles** is as extravagant as the Sun King was himself. A visit to the château takes most or all of a day and entails a lot of walking. Versailles is 24km (15 miles) southwest of Paris, by road (N10); by train from Gare St-Lazare to Versailles; by RER (line C5) to Versailles-Rive Gauche; or by Métro to Pont de Sèvres, then bus 171. Palace: Tue–Sun 9am–5.30pm, Apr–Oct until 6.30pm. Marie Antoinette's Estate (incl. Petit Trianon) and Grand Trianon: daily noon–5.30pm, Apr–Oct until 7pm. Gardens: daily Apr–Oct 7am–sunset (except when the musical extravaganzas 'Grandes Eaux Musicales' are held, see website for details), Nov–Mar 8am–sunset; www.chateauversailles.fr.

Highlights of the interior include: the baroque **Royal Chapel**; the **State Apartments**, in which Louis XIV entertained; the Salon de Diane, where he played billiards; the 73-m (240-ft) long **Galerie des Glaces** (Hall of Mirrors); and the King's Bedroom, where Louis died of gangrene in 1715. In the Queen's Bedroom, 19 royal children were born, the births often attended by members of the court, as was the custom.

The grandest facade faces west to the gardens, where the fountains begin to play at 3.30pm on three Sundays a month (May–Sept). The **Grand Trianon**, the small palace Louis XIV used when he wanted to escape the vast château; the **Petit Trianon**, favoured by Louis XV; and the **Hameau** and miniature farm, where Louis XVI's queen, Marie-Antoinette, reputedly played at being a country girl, are also worth a visit.

Fontainebleau

The seat of sovereigns from Louis IX to Napoleon III and a glittering example of French Mannerism, the château at
Fontainebleau (Wed–Mon 9.30am–5pm, June–Sept until 36
6pm, last admission 45 mins before closing, www.musee-chateau-fontainebleau.fr) makes a pleasant day trip from Paris. Here Louis XIV signed the Revocation of the Edict of Nantes in 1685, and Napoleon I signed his first act of abdication in 1814. More recently (1945–65) Fontainebleau was the headquarters of the military branch of NATO. Fontainebleau is 64km (40 miles) southeast of Paris by the A6 or by train from Gare de Lyon, then bus to the château.

The château at Fontainebleau

Malmaison

Set in lovely grounds, the château at **Malmaison** (Wed–Mon Apr–Sept 10am–5.45pm, Sat–Sun until 6.15pm, Oct–Mar 10am–12.30pm and 1.30–5.15pm, Sat–Sun until 5.45pm, www.chateau-malmaison.fr) was the home of Napoleon's wife, Josephine, who continued to live here after their divorce. Many of her possessions are on display. Malmaison is 6km (4 miles) west of Paris. Métro: Grande Arche de La Défense, then bus 258, or RER to Rueil-Malmaison, followed by a walk or short taxi ride.

37 Vaux-le-Vicomte

This 17th-century château (mid-Mar–mid-Nov daily 10am–1pm and 2–6pm, candlelit visits May–mid-Oct Sat 8pm–midnight, also Fri in July–Aug, www.vaux-le-vicomte.com) was designed by Louis Le Vau, André Le Nôtre and Charles Le Brun for Louis XIV's finance minister, Fouquet. No sooner was it completed than the king had its owner arrested for embezzlement and jailed for life. **Vaux-le-Vicomte** is 55km (35 miles) southeast of Paris on the N5 or by train from Gare de Lyon to Melun, then a taxi ride.

Giverny

Claude Monet lived at this house in **Giverny** (Apr–Oct daily 9.30am–6pm, last admission 5.30pm, www.fondation-monet.com) from 1883 to 1926 and painted the gardens many times, especially the water lilies. Giverny is situated 85km (53 miles) northwest of Paris by the A13, D181 and D5, or by train from Gare St-Lazare to Vernon, with a shuttle bus from the station to Giverny.

Disneyland Paris

Disney's ambitious recreation complex encompasses hotels, restaurants, a convention centre, a golf course, tennis courts

Monet's *Bridge over a Pool ofWater Lilies*

and several swimming pools – and attracts over 12 million visitors a year. In the theme park itself, Main Street USA recaptures the traditions of small-town America at the turn of the 20th century, and leads to four other 'lands' – Frontierland, Adventureland, Fantasyland and Discoveryland. Each themed section has a variety of fun experiences to offer. Hosts Mickey and Minnie Mouse, Goofy, Donald Duck and Pluto wander around in their familiar costumes, posing with visitors. Every day at 3pm there's a parade including floats inspired by the famous Disney movies. In the **Walt Disney Studios Park** visitors can explore film sets; the newest thrill ride, the Twilight Zone Tower of Terror, ends with a sheer drop into a black hole.

The resort is 32km (20 miles) east of Paris, near Marne-la-Vallée. A motorway gives access from the city and the airports, Charles-de-Gaulle and Orly. Speedy commuter trains (RPEER line A) from the capital and even faster long-distance trains (TGV) serve Marne-la-Vallée/Chessy station near the entrance.

8e Arrt
RUE
DU FAUBOURG
SAINT HONORÉ
LANVIN

WHAT TO DO

Sightseeing in Paris is only part of the pleasure of a visit. Its shops, ranging from high-end boutiques and speciality stores to flea markets, are among the best in the world. The town also provides plenty of opportunities for fitness enthusiasts and fans of spectator sports. As for cultural entertainment, the city offers an enormous variety of plays, films and music.

SHOPPING

One sure way to appreciate the city's beauty and character is to window-shop on elegant place Vendôme, meander along boulevard St-Germain, rummage through the book stalls on the banks of the Seine or peer into the eccentric dens of the covered passages. Paris has a wonderful variety of shops, and there is still a strong tradition of small specialist retailers.

What to Buy Where

Each of Paris's *quartiers* has its own mood and atmosphere, and the shops often reflect its history and the type of people who live there. In terms of fashion, expect boho designers in hilly Montmartre; designer couture along avenue Montaigne and rue du Faubourg-St-Honoré; and cool, contemporary streetwear around Les Halles and rue Etienne-Marcel.

Other areas take a bit more delving into: the exclusive residential western sector of the 7th *arrondissement* is good for traditional menswear and equipment for the golfing brigade, along with

Gourmet paradise

Paris is a remarkably well-fed city, and every *quartier* has its chocolatiers, superb patisseries and boulangeries, delicatessens, ripe-smelling cheese shops and bustling street markets.

Department store Printemps

upmarket interior design boutiques and furnishing fabrics. Chic place Vendôme is where you'll find diamond-encrusted baubles, but you'll find more original pieces in St-Germain or the Marais. Similarly, whereas opulent 18th-century antiques are sold around quai Voltaire in the 7th and rue du Faubourg-St-Honoré in the 8th, retro furnishing and ceramics from the 1960s and 1970s are popular near Bastille or Montmartre.

This said, the shopping map of Paris is far from static, reflecting an ebb and flow that goes with the rise and fall of different areas. The Champs-Elysées, which zigzagged from the epitome of glamour in the early 20th century to that of tourist dross in the 1980s, started returning to favour with a vengeance at the end of the 1990s, and is now buzzing with upmarket brands and a new multi-brand store, LE66. Long-staid rue St-Honoré is now the focus for a more avant-garde fashion set, chasing trends at concept store Colette. Similarly, in the past few years, designer fashion has migrated to once-literary St-Germain, to the chagrin of those who bemoan the disappearance of favourite bookshops and food stores.

Whereas the Marais was first fashionable in the early 17th century, it fell into decline with the departure of Louis XIV and his court to Versailles, and only began its slow recovery in the 1960s. But since the 1990s, restoration of its beautiful *hôtels particuliers* and the installation of several important museums have turned the area into a highly international district with many youthful fashion boutiques and quirky gift shops.

A parallel specialist enclave is the Marais's gay area, with its hub around the attractive rue Vieille-du-Temple. The past few years have seen the arrival of not just bars, but gay-oriented bookshops and clothing stores, often replacing Jewish bookshops and bakeries in what had long been a Jewish district.

Other areas reflect the changing population of Paris. In the 13th *arrondissement,* in the 'Chinatown' quarter with its large South-East Asian population, you'll find Chinese supermarkets and *patisseries* among the high-rise tower blocks. Other previously overlooked territories have arrived on the retail map, notably along the Canal St-Martin, where women's fashion retailer Antoine et Lili has set up three colourful, kitsch shops.

Other *quartiers* have not fared quite as well: Les Halles seems to be in perpetual decline, with its flagging array of unappealing, brash chain stores and dodgy reputation, and the aristocratic past of boulevards Bonne Nouvelle and Montmartre is a distant memory blurred by the ranks of discount stores and fast-food chains there.

Galerie Vivienne

Markets

Paris's markets pull in bargain hunters, gourmets and collectors alike. There are three fleamarkets: on the outskirts, the classy Marché de St-Ouen and the smaller Marché de Montreuil and, in the 12th *arrondissement*, the Marché d'Aligre. 'Roving' street markets are held two or three mornings a week (7am–2.30pm); at these you may find the most authentic produce and a local flavour that varies from *quartier* to *quartier*.

In addition there are over 50 street markets; some have just a few stalls, whereas others, such as Marché Bastille or avenue Daumesnil, stretch for hundreds of metres and have a superb range of stock. Market streets, including rue Mouffetard, in the Latin Quarter, have food shops with stalls that spill on to the pavement and are open all day from Tuesday to Saturday, with a long break for lunch, and on Sunday morning. For a full list with opening times, see 'Les marchés parisiens' at www.paris.fr.

Chic fashions on avenue Montaigne

SPORTS

The city caters fairly well for the sports enthusiast. You can find details on sporting events in the Wednesday edition of *Le Figaro*. For information (in French) on sporting facilities, contact Allô-Sports (tel: 08 20 00 75 75).

Spectator Sports

Football and rugby fans can watch games at the huge **Stade de France** just north of the city ringroad. The stadium (rue Francis de Pressensé, St-Denis, tel: 01 55 93 00 00, www.stade france.com, daily 10am–6pm, except when events are taking place) is also used for rock concerts, seating 100,000 spectators. The Parc des Princes in the 16th *arrondissement* is home to Paris's premier division football team, Paris St-Germain. The huge **Palais Omnisports Paris Bercy** (8 boulevard de Bercy, 75012, tel: 01 44 68 44 68, www.bercy.fr) hosts events including football, ice sports, motor sports and horse riding.

For racing, the Grand Prix de l'Arc de Triomphe takes place in October, at Longchamp in the Bois de Boulogne.

Participant Sports

The few public tennis courts in Paris, such as those at the Jardin du Luxembourg, are available on a first-come-first-served basis. Municipal swimming pools include the new Piscine Josephine Baker that floats on the Seine. For details of municipal sports facilities, see www.sport.paris.fr. The Bois de Boulogne, quais de Seine and Canal St-Martin offer good cycling opportunities; the Fédération Française de Cyclotourisme, tel: 01 44 16 88 88, has details of cycling clubs.

Sporting events

Major sporting events include the Six Nations Cup in Feb/March, the Marathon in April, and the French Tennis Open in May/June at the Stade Roland-Garros.

ENTERTAINMENT

For listings of what's on in Paris, buy one of the weekly guides, *Pariscope* or *L'Officiel des Spectacles*, both of which come out on Wednesday. *Figaroscope*, the Wednesday supplement of *Le Figaro* newspaper, is another good source of information. The tourist office also has up-to-date event information (in several languages). See also www.paris-info.com.

Theatre

The main national theatre is the state-funded **Comédie Française** (1 place Colette, 75001, tel: 01 44 58 15 15, www.comedie-francaise.fr), where works by such revered writers as Molière and Racine are performed. Modern classics are shown here and at its sister theatre, the Théâtre du Vieux Colombier (21 rue du Vieux-Colombier, 75006, http://vieux.colombier.free.fr); the Théâtre du Châtelet (2 rue Edouard Colonne, 75001, www.chatelet-theatre.com), run by Paris city hall, hosts opera, classical concerts and the occasional ballet.

Cinema

Paris has numerous multi-screen cinemas showing the latest blockbusters, but if you'd rather see a French classic, there are a number of good art-house cinemas too. Most cinemas in the centre of Paris show films in their original language with sub-titles in French ('VO' – *version originale*), though once you get out of the city centre, mainstream films are usually dubbed ('VF' – *version française*). For a unique cinematic experience visit **La Pagode** (57bis rue de Babylone, 75007, tel: 01 45 55 48 48), where the latest films are shown in an exotic Japanese setting complete with a tea room. Cinema buffs can also pay homage at the **Cinémathèque Française**, 51 rue de Bercy, 75012, www.cinematheque.fr, in a Cubist building by Frank Gehry.

Music and Ballet

'Little sparrow' Edith Piaf

Opera and **ballet** are staged in the lavish Palais Garnier (place de l'Opéra) and in the modern Opéra Bastille (2bis place de la Bastille). For details visit www.operadeparis.fr.

Paris has many jazz clubs. An established venue is the Caveau de la Huchette (5 rue de la Huchette, www.caveau delahuchette.fr). Le Sunset/ Sunside (60 rue des Lombards, www.sunset-sunside.com) is two jazz clubs in one: electric jazz and world music, plus acoustic. Bigger names perform at New Morning (rue des Petites-Ecuries) and the Lionel Hampton club at the Méridien Etoile (Porte Maillot).

Pop and rock concerts are held at the Zénith in the Parc de la Villette *(see page 65)*, Parc des Princes (Métro: Porte de St-Cloud) and the Palais Omnisports Paris Bercy *(see page 95)*. Ticket offices *(billeteries)* at branches of the Fnac books and records chain or Virgin Megastore on the Champs-Elysées will have details of what groups are in town.

Cabarets

Lavish floor shows, geared mainly towards tourists, hark back to the 'naughty' image of Paris of yesteryear. The Lido (116bis avenue des Champs-Elysées) and the Folies Bergères (32 rue Richer), which launched Josephine Baker, Mistinguett and Maurice Chevalier, are classic survivors. The Crazy Horse (12 avenue George V) puts on slick erotic shows. The Moulin Rouge (82 boulevard de Clichy) puts on two shows a night.

A night out in the Marais

Clubs and Bars

Keeping up with the latest in clubs can be a full-time job for dedicated night-owls. Many are nominally private, meaning you only get in if your face fits.

The words 'Paris nightlife' make many visitors think of Montmartre and Montparnasse, but these days the biggest after-dark buzz is around rue Oberkampf in the east of the city. **Café Charbon** (109 rue Oberkampf, 75011, www.nouveaucasino.net) launched the area's nightlife boom nearly two decades ago, and is still going strong; behind it is the same management's **Nouveau Casino**, one of the liveliest nightclubs in the city. A more recent arrival is nearby **L'Alimentation Générale** (64 rue Jean-Pierre Timbaud, 75011, tel: 01 43 55 42 50), a cavernous bar with a drinks menu featuring plenty of unusual bottled beers and innovative cocktails.

Exciting new venues are not confined to the east. **Showcase** (Pont Alexandre III, 75008, www.showcase.fr) is one of the city's most recent nightlife venues, a gorgeous club underneath the Right Bank end of the Pont Alexandre III that attracts a trendy young crowd. Also in the eighth arrondissement is the famous **Black Calavados** (40 avenue Pierre Ier de Serbie, www.bc-paris.fr). It's not cheap, but it certainly is glamorous.

In the centre of town, another iconic drinking den is **Harry's Bar** (5 rue Daunou, 75002, www.harrys-bar.fr). This authentic Paris institution was frequented by Hemingway (naturally), Gershwin and others; it claims to have invented the Bloody Mary, no less. The cocktails are excellent – and strong.

Further north, and with a more youthful, electro vibe, is **Point Ephémère** (200 quai de Valmy, 75010, www.point ephemere.org), set on the bank of the Canal St-Martin a short walk south-west from Jaurès métro station. This expansive clubbing and concert venue also has a good restaurant and café, a waterfront terrace in summer, and a gallery.

The Marais is where to hang out for the gay scene, with institutions like **Le Central** and **Le Cox Bar**, and the rue des Ecouffes, peppered with lesbian bars, cafés and boutiques.

CHILDREN

For most children, Disneyland *(see page 88)* will probably appeal far more than city sightseeing. For a cheaper alternative, an afternoon in one of Paris's parks *(see pages 41 and 75)* might do the trick. For small children there are merry-go-rounds, puppet theatres (not July and August), pony rides and toy boats in the **Jardin du Luxembourg**. Animal-loving younsters may like to visit the **Jardin d'Acclimatation** *(see page 61)*, a children's park with a zoo, pony rides and puppet shows in the Bois de Boulogne. For the scientifically minded, there's a lot to learn in the **Cité des Sciences et de l'Industrie** *(see page 65)*; there's also a hands-on approach at the **Palais de la Découverte** *(see page 57)*.

Calendar of Events

For details of these and other events, see www.parisinfo.com.

January Prêt à Porter Paris, the spring ready-to-wear fashion shows at Paris-Expo, Métro: Porte de Versailles. Chinese New Year, Chinatown, 13th *arrondissement*, Métro: Porte d'Ivry.

Spring Foire du Trône (late March–early May), a monster funfair at Pelouse de Reuilly, Bois de Vincennes, Métro: Porte Dorée.

April Paris Marathon ends on the Champs-Elysées.

Good Friday Archbishop of Paris leads Procession of the Cross up the steps of Sacré-Coeur basilica, Montmartre, Métro: Anvers.

May/June French Open Tennis Championships, chic Grand Slam event, Roland-Garros stadium, Métro: Porte d'Auteuil.

June For the Fête de la Musique (Music Festival) on the 21st, there are free concerts all over Paris. The Course des Garçons et Serveuses de Café has 500 waiters and waitresses racing through the *grands boulevards* and St-Germain-des-Près.

July Bastille Day (14th). Festivities include a colourful military parade along the Champs-Elysées, a firework display at the Trocadéro and dancing on place de la Bastille. The Tour de France ends on the Champs-Elysées. Paris Cinéma, international film festival, screenings at various venues; see www.paris-cinema.org. Night-time firework displays and illuminated fountains at the Château de Versailles (July–Sept).

September Journées du Patrimoine, open days at otherwise off-limits government and private buildings.

October Prix de l'Arc de Triomphe, France's biggest horse race, Longchamp, Bois de Boulogne, Métro: Porte d'Auteuil and free shuttle-bus. Festival d'Automne, the annual festival of theatre, music and dance (until December).

November The arrival of Beaujolais Nouveau (third Tuesday of the month) is celebrated in bars and restaurants.

December Notre-Dame cathedral is packed for 11pm Christmas Eve Mass. New Year's Eve crowds pour onto the Champs-Elysées, and there are fireworks at the Trocadéro.

EATING OUT

Paris has the reputation of being one of the best culinary cities in the world. However, over the past ten years food critics have been hard on the French capital, claiming that, unlike in London, New York and Sydney, the dining scene has been stubbornly slow to evolve. There is some truth to these reproaches – France is conservative when it comes to food – but this attitude is not without benefits, especially for visitors.

Classic to Contemporary

The great cuisines of the world can be counted on one hand, and French cuisine is one of them. What the term implies is an established, coherent body of ingredients, techniques and dishes, which have all been studied and perfected by masters of

Red gingham – traditional French dining

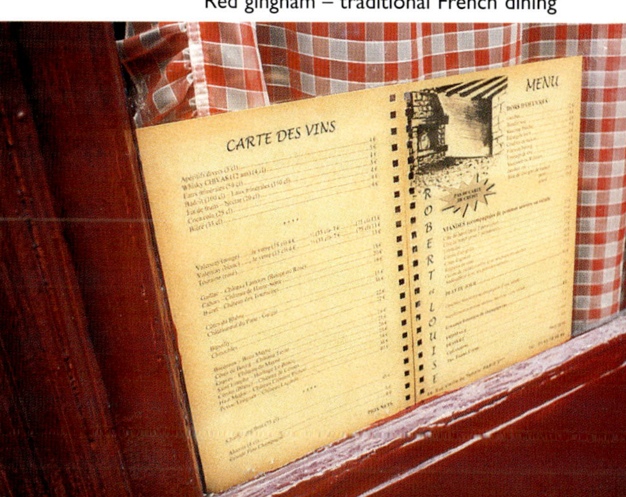

Le Train Bleu at Gare de Lyon

the art over many years. So, if a chef doesn't immediately put lemongrass in his *coq au vin*, it doesn't necessarily mean that he's unimaginative: it simply means that he respects tradition and has enough experience to know the risks. In other words, it could be argued that French cuisine went through its culinary adolescence long ago, and that at this stage there are some taste thrills it considers not worth pursuing.

This is not to say that French food isn't evolving. New flavours are integrated into the cooking all the time, albeit carefully. Curry, lime, peanut, peppers, coconut and lemongrass are all common on gastronomic menus. Most dishes remain French at the core, but exotic nuances are certainly part of the high-end experience. In the middle ground, couscous is eaten almost as often as *boeuf bourguignon*, and sushi seems to be the city's favourite fast food.

Even in terms of technique, French cooking has modernised; sauces and pastries, for example, tend to be lighter than they were previously, and vegetables are more prevalent on menus. Menus themselves have been simplified – better aligned to contemporary appetites. Still, it's a slow-and-steady-wins-the-race approach to moving cuisine forward.

The advantage of this from a visitor's perspective is that the classic dishes we dream about can still be found in authentic form on French tables. If you want French onion soup, you can find it, plain and simple. If you order *steak au poivre*, out will come that desired slab of beef in a creamy, peppery sauce that spills across the plate towards your crispy pile of *frites*. There are even a few bistros left where old-style service is still the norm, so when you order, say, *mousse au chocolat*, you'll be given a family-sized bowl from which you can serve yourself until you swear that you'll never want to see the dish again as long as you live.

There's still plenty of mediocrity as far as restaurant food goes, but the French are so French about it all that sometimes even the most ghastly meals can have a certain charm.

Another thing that makes French food extraordinary (and the bad French food, on a gracious day, forgivable) is the degree to which it is social. Even with the increased pace of modern life, the French still believe in sitting down and sharing meals in good company over a bottle of wine. They take time to eat – they make time. In fact, food in France, more than just sustenance, is a lifestyle; and this, if nothing else, is something you'll wish you could pack in your bag and take home with you when you leave.

Le Fooding

The term 'Le Fooding', coined in 1999 by journalist Alexandre Cammas, joins the two English words 'food' and 'feeling' to express an attitude towards dining that emphasises emotion, atmosphere, alluring food presentation, imagination, entertainment and time, as much as high-quality food on the plate. Says Cammas, 'People need a lot more than just good food to feel well fed.' It's all about approaching the table with the mind and all the senses, not just an empty belly and a greedy tongue. In a way, this is what France has always been famous for. For restaurants that share these ideals, visit www.lefooding.com.

Where to Eat

Eateries in Paris are still by and large French: bistros, brasseries, cafés and haute-cuisine restaurants. Bistros tend to serve simple, traditional dishes. The food quality varies from one to the next, unlike the menus, which are practically carbon copies of each other: potato and herring salad, duck confit, beef daube, chocolate mousse and tarte Tatin – over and over and over again. Brasseries (the louder, brighter, Belle Epoque option) offer a range of bistro dishes, but also specialise in seafood – heaps of oysters, mussels, langoustines, lobsters and clams spinning past on waiters' dexterous palms – and Alsatian dishes including choucroute and plenty of beer.

Cafés, in the traditional sense of the term, usually serve sandwiches, notably the classic *croque-monsieur* (grilled ham and cheese) and a variety of salads. However, modern cafés – trendy, chic establishments that pack in fashionable crowds – serve full menus, typically of contemporary, cosmopolitan food with a Mediterranean bent.

At the high end, Michelin-starred restaurants range from being gloriously old-fashioned, with truffle-studded foie gras terrines and venison in grand old sauces, to being acrobatically cutting-edge with hot pepper sorbets to cleanse the palate between veal slow-cooked in orange juice and desserts that show off milk or chocolate in five different ways. One of the best ways to enjoy the starred places is to opt for a tasting menu *(dégustation)*, which affords you hours at the table tasting a host of dishes in smaller-than-usual portions, so there's room for them all.

Generally speaking, restaurants serve lunch from noon–

Ordering water

Several varieties of mineral water *(eau minérale)* may be on offer in French restaurants. Request *pétillante* for lightly sparkling, *gazeuse* if you want carbonated water, *plate* for still, or *en carafe*, if a jug of water from the tap suits you.

Art Nouveau décor at Gallopin

2.30 or 3pm and dinner from around 7 or 8–10.30 or 11pm, although this may vary, particularly in August, when many establishments shut for the summer.

Ethnic Cuisine

If you get to the point where you think you might burst if you have to look at another plate of French food, take a break by seeking out some of the city's international restaurants. What better way to experience the different *quartiers* of Paris than through the city's exceptional – and delicious – culinary scene? Paris is especially good for food from Morocco, other parts of Africa, the Antilles, Thailand, Vietnam and Japan. In terms of location, the greatest concentration of Chinese and Vietnamese restaurants is in the 5th and 13th *arrondissements* (roughly speaking, the Latin Quarter and southeast to the new Left Bank), and Japanese restaurants are numerous in parts of the 1st (especially on and around rue Ste-Anne). The

Le Square Trousseau in the 12th *arrondissement*

best Moroccan restaurants are dotted across the capital, but around the Bastille is a good place to start from. There is excellent Lebanese food in the 8th and 16th (Madeleine, Grands Boulevards, Champs-Elysées and West), and good African food can be found around Pigalle and the East.

Eating Out with Children

Taking your children out to a restaurant should not be a problem (although check beforehand with the more upmarket places). French children are used to eating out from an early age and are therefore generally well behaved in restaurants. Many establishments offer a children's menu. If not, they may split a *prix fixe* menu between two. With very young children, just request an extra plate and give them food from your own. With the bread that should come automatically to a French table, and ice-cream or fruit to follow, most children will be well fed.

TO HELP YOU ORDER

Do you have a table?	**Avez-vous une table?**
The bill, please	**L'addition, s'il vous plaît**
I would like ...	**J'aimerais...**

tea	**du thé**	pepper	**du poivre**
coffee	**un café**	salad	**une salade**
milk	**du lait**	soup	**de la soupe**
sugar	**du sucre**	fish	**du poisson**
wine	**du vin**	seafood	**des fruits de mer**
beer	**une bière**		
water	**de l'eau**	meat	**de la viande**
bread	**du pain**	very rare	**bleu**
butter	**du beurre**	rare	**saignant**
cheese	**du fromage**	medium-rare	**rose**
chips (fries)	**des frites**	medium	**à point**
salt	**du sel**	well done	**bien cuit**

MENU READER

agneau	lamb	**jambon**	ham
ail	garlic	**moules**	mussels
bœuf	beef	**œufs**	eggs
canard	duck	**oignons**	onions
champignons	mushrooms	**petits pois**	peas
chou	cabbage	**poire**	pear
choufleur	cauliflower	**pomme**	apple
crevettes roses/grises	prawns/ shrimps	**pomme de terre**	potato
dinde	turkey	**porc**	pork
épinards	spinach	**poulet**	chicken
escargots	snails	**riz**	rice
fraises	strawberries	**saucisse**	sausage
framboises	raspberries	**saumon**	salmon
haricots verts	green beans	**thon**	tuna
huîtres	oysters	**veau**	veal

PLACES TO EAT

We have used the following symbols to give an idea of the price for a three-course meal for one, including a glass of house wine, tax and service:

€€€€ over 80 euros	**€€** 30–50 euros
€€€ 50–80 euros	**€** below 30 euros

THE RIGHT BANK

LOUVRE AND TUILERIES

Café Marly €€–€€€ *Palais du Louvre, 93 rue de Rivoli, 75001, tel: 01 49 26 06 60.* Open daily for lunch and dinner (until 2am). Rest from your labours at the Louvre in the lavish Second Empire-style rooms facing the Pyramid or on the attractive covered terrace. This café is popular with the fashionable set and tends to be busy. Modern European cooking. Nice for breakfast.

Costes €€€€ *239 rue St-Honoré, 75001, tel: 01 42 44 50 25.* Open daily 7am–1am. This restaurant in the chic Hotel Costes is one of the most popular upmarket venues in Paris. Beautiful courtyard, baroque interior and an eclectic menu. Reserve.

Le Fumoir €€–€€€ *6 rue de l'Amiral-de-Coligny, 75001, tel: 01 42 92 00 24.* Open daily for lunch and dinner; brunch on Sunday. With an admirable location facing the Louvre, spacious, sophisticated Le Fumoir is renowned for shaking some of the best cocktails in town. It serves light pan-European cooking, such as monkfish with peas and asparagus and sea bass with ginger.

Le Grand Véfour €€€€ *17 rue de Beaujolais, 75001, tel: 01 42 96 56 27.* Open Mon–Fri for lunch, Mon–Thurs for dinner. Set under the arches of the Palais-Royal is one of the most beautiful restaurants in Paris. Le Grand Véfour opened its doors in 1784 and has fed the likes of Emperor Napoléon and writers Alphonse Lamartine and Victor Hugo. Today it serves haute cuisine in the hands of chef Guy Martin.

GRANDS BOULEVARDS

Alain Ducasse au Plaza Athénée €€€€ *25 avenue Montaigne, 75008, tel: 01 53 67 65 00.* Open for lunch Thurs–Fri, dinner Mon–Fri. Cooking elevated to an art form from France's first recipient of six Michelin stars (three apiece for two restaurants). Expect truffles in abundance and superb vegetables from Provence. The listed neo-rococo decor has been rejuvenated with ethereal glittery crystals. Reserve well ahead.

Angl'Opéra €€€ *39 avenue de l'Opéra, 75008, tel: 01 42 61 86 25.* Michelin-starred chef Gilles Choukroun turns out daring, but delicious, creations in the funky restaurant of the Hôtel Edouard VII *(see page 135)*. A good choice if you've overdosed on traditional French fare.

Café de la Paix €€–€€€ *place de l'Opéra, 75009, tel: 01 40 07 36 36.* Open daily for lunch and dinner. The main reason to come here is the historic setting of this 1862 café; it's vast, gilded and mirrored, adjoining a covered terrace opposite the Palais Garnier.

Chartier € *7 rue du Faubourg-Montmartre, 75009, tel: 01 47 70 86 29.* Open for lunch and dinner Mon–Sat. The best-known low-price eaterie in town. The ambience is an experience in itself: Belle Epoque decor, snappy waiters, shared tables and plenty of *bonhomie.* Arrive before 1pm or before 8pm at night or you may not get a seat.

Gallopin €€€ *40 rue Notre-Dame-des-Victoires 75002, tel: 01 42 36 45 38.* Open for lunch and dinner Mon–Sat. This famous brasserie opened in 1876 and is still decorated in elegant Belle Epoque style. The chef prepares refined versions of traditional dishes, including *pâté maison*, grilled meats and flambéed *crêpes.* The fish is a star attraction, with specialities such as haddock poached in milk with fresh spinach, and deliciously fresh seafood platters.

Ladurée €€ *75 avenue des Champs-Elysées, 75008, tel: 01 40 75 08 75.* Open daily 8am–1am. Renowned in Paris for generations for its delectable macaroons, this café/bakery/restaurant is always busy and very chic. Excellent puff pastry filled with veal and mushrooms, and baked cod with candied lemon. Desserts are a particular strength, especially the melt-in-the-mouth macaroons. There's also a branch at 16 rue Royale.

Spoon €€ *14 rue de Marignan 75008, tel: 01 40 76 34 44*. Open weekdays for lunch and dinner. The prototype of Ducasse's mix-and-match global kitchens draws a hot mix of media, fashion and showbiz types. The restaurant has two personalities, as white linen shades on the dining room walls are raised in the evening to reveal purple upholstered walls. Desserts are often of American inspiration. Book ahead.

CHAMPS-ELYSEES AND TROCADÉRO

L'Appart €€–€€€ *9–11 rue du Colisée, 75008, tel: 01 53 75 42 00*. Open daily for lunch and dinner; Sunday brunch. Close to the Champs-Elysées, this modern bistro looks more like someone's apartment (hence the name) with shelves of books lining the walls. The cooking is creative but not fussy: think colourful salads, candied aubergine, veal with mustard seeds, and fresh cod with mashed potatoes. Reasonably priced wines.

Tokyo Eat €€ *Palais de Tokyo, 13 avenue du Président Wilson, 75016, tel: 01 47 20 00 29*. Open for lunch and dinner Tue–Sun An airy space with open kitchen and funky lighting. The menu skips from global satays and unusual carpaccios to roast chicken. The terrace is open in summer.

BEAUBOURG, MARAIS, BASTILLE AND EAST

L'Apparemment Café € *18 rue des Coutures-St-Gervais, 75003, tel: 01 48 87 12 22*. Open daily 9am–1am. Stepping inside this quaint café near the Musée Picasso is like entering someone's house. Cosy seats make for lovely lazy dining, and simple, tasty food. There are board games, too.

L'As du Fallafel € *34 rue des Rosiers, 75004, tel: 01 48 87 63 60*. Open Sun–Fri noon–midnight, closed Sat. The best *falafel* in

Paris is a meal in itself. There are also *shawarma* sandwiches in pitta bread. Great location in the heart of the Marais.

Brasserie Bofinger €€–€€€ *5–7 rue de la Bastille, 75004, tel: 01 42 72 87 82*. Open daily for lunch and dinner. Close to the Opéra Bastille, the huge (300-seater) Bofinger is the archetypal Belle Epoque brasserie, complete with lush red-and-gold decor. It's a great place in which to experience brasserie fare: delicious oysters and seafood and specialities from Alsace such as *choucroute*. Excellent service.

Chai 33 €€–€€€ *33 cour St-Emilion, 75012, tel: 01 53 44 01 01*. Open daily for lunch and dinner. Innovative restaurant set in a light, airy former wine warehouse in hip Bercy. Choose your wine according to six styles, from light with a bite to rich and silky, with refreshing fusion food to match. Unpretentious *sommeliers* are on hand to help with wine choices. Fun.

Chez Prune €–€€ *71 quai Valmy, 75010, tel: 01 42 41 30 47*. Open daily for lunch and dinner. A cornerstone of the trendy Canal St-Martin area. This is still one of the better places in Paris from which to watch the world go by. Good food at lunchtime; tapas-style snacks at night.

Le Petit Fer à Cheval € *30 rue Vieille-du-Temple, 75004, tel: 01 42 72 47 47*. Open daily for lunch and dinner. People-watching is as much a full-time occupation here as it is anywhere else along the Marais's trendy rue Vieille-du-Temple. With its tiny horseshoe-shaped bar, this café is atmospheric and a great favourite with the bourgeois-bohemian crowd. Decent food. Friendly service.

Le Petit Marcel €–€€ *65 rue Rambuteau, 75004, tel: 01 48 87 10 20*. Open daily for lunch and dinner (until 12am). This formerly postage stamp-sized bistro – now expanded – near the Centre Pompidou is as quaint as it gets, with attractive Art Nouveau tiles. The locals will grab the few terrace seats first, but inside, beneath the painted ceiling on a rickety chair, you're just as much part of the scene. Salads, omelettes, steak frites, tarte Tatin: basic food, but decent, cheap and delightful. No credit cards.

Le Square Trousseau €€–€€€ *1 rue Antoine-Vollon, 75012, tel: 01 43 43 06 00*. Open Tue–Sat for lunch and dinner. It's no surprise that this bistro has been used for film sets: it's spacious, with Art Deco lamps, colourful tiles and a glamorous bar. In summer, diners squeeze on to the terrace facing a leafy square. Gazpacho, tuna tartare, rosemary lamb and spring vegetables, beef with shallot sauce, and raspberry gratin are among the delights available.

Train Bleu €€ *Gare de Lyon, 750012, tel: 01 43 43 09 06*. Open daily for lunch and dinner. Built over a century ago in the midst of the Gare de Lyon, this huge, lavish-looking restaurant is considered an artistic marvel, with frescoed ceilings, mosaics and Belle Epoque murals. Classic French dishes are served quickly and efficiently. Good-value set menus.

WESTERN PARIS

Guy Savoy €€€€ *18 rue Troyon, 75017, tel: 01 43 80 40 61*. Open for lunch Tue–Fri, dinner Tue–Sat. It took some time for Savoy's imaginative haute cuisine to finally earn the highest Michelin rating, belated recognition of one of Paris's most inventive chefs. The son of a gardener, Savoy has an obsession with vegetables that anticipated the recent trend by more than a decade. He happily pairs truffles with lentils or artichokes, and regularly makes the rounds to greet his guests.

Pré Catelan €€€€ *route de Suresnes, 75016, tel: 01 44 14 41 14*. Open for lunch and dinner Tue–Sat, lunch only on Sun. Situated in the heart of the Bois de Boulogne, this is one of the most romantic spots in Paris. Haute cuisine centring on fresh truffles, lobster, lamb and fresh seafood. The pastry chef is considered one of the best in France. Call well ahead to book a table.

MONTMARTRE AND THE NORTHEAST

Au Grain de Folie € *24 rue de la Vieuville, 75018, tel: 01 42 58 15 57*. Open for lunch and dinner Mon–Sat, non-stop Sun 12.30–11pm. A self-styled 'vegetarian place for non-vegetarians', this is a quaint spot for a healthy bite on your way to the Butte. Sit at a check-cloth-covered table and enjoy a bowl of homemade soup, a crispy vegetable platter, or a slice of savoury tart. A tight squeeze but friendly atmosphere.

Casa Olympe €€ *48 rue St-Georges, 75009, tel: 01 42 85 26 01.* Open Mon–Fri for lunch and dinner (closed first three weeks in Aug). Olympe Versini is one of Paris's best-known female chefs, and in this no-frills dining room she offers a limited but strong menu. Classic French dishes such as *steak tartare* hit the spot.

Chez Toinette €€ *20 rue Germain-Pilon, 75018, tel: 01 42 54 44 36.* With its red walls and romantic lighting, this cosy and convivial bistro in the heights of Montmartre is a good bet for a classic French lunch or dinner. Try the wild boar terrine, and don't miss the superb crème brûlée.

THE LEFT BANK

LATIN QUARTER AND ST-GERMAIN-DES-PRÉS

L'Alcazar €€–€€€ *62 rue Mazarine, 75006, tel: 01 53 10 19 99.* Open daily for lunch and dinner, brunch on Sun. Sir Terence Conran's contribution to the Paris restaurant scene was to transform this former musical hall into a designer brasserie. It's been a hit, thanks to the easygoing atmosphere and competitively priced menu, which includes an upmarket interpretation of British fish and chips.

Allard €€–€€€ *41 rue St-André des Arts, 75006, tel: 01 43 26 48 23.* The dark, Art Nouveau decoration makes this one of the loveliest bistros in Paris, with two small but intimate and atmospheric rooms evocative of Left Bank life. The traditional food – think duck with olives, roasted lamb, etc – is very good.

Angelina's €€–€€€ *226 rue de Rivoli, 75001, tel: 01 42 60 82 00.* Famed Paris tearoom that is also good for lunch. Serves great squishy meringues.

L'Atelier de Joël Robuchon €€€€ *5 rue Montalembert, 75007, tel: 01 42 22 56 56.* Open daily for lunch and dinner. Even jaded

Parisians queue up in all weathers to sample the warm *foie gras brochettes* or tapenade with fresh tuna conjured by France's most revered chef. The restaurant is built around an open kitchen, so you can watch the masters at work, and the atmosphere is slick, like that of a bar. Reservations are accepted for first seatings only (11.30am and 6.30pm). No smoking.

Brasserie Lipp €€–€€€ *151 boulevard St-Germain, 75006, tel: 01 45 48 53 91*. Open daily for lunch and dinner until 1am. Everyone who's anyone in St-Germain-des-Prés has a table here. Not to be missed for a view of the neighbourhood eccentrics. Brasserie fare (Alsace country cooking), notably stews and *choucroute* (sauerkraut). Reasonably priced house Riesling.

La Closerie des Lilas €€–€€€ *171 boulevard du Montparnasse, 75006, tel: 01 40 51 34 50*. Open daily for lunch and dinner. Spiritual home to Left Bank intellectuals, the Closerie remains one of the most attractive institutions in the city. There's a reliable brasserie, a more expensive restaurant (great French classics) and a lovely bar.

La Ferrandaise €€ *8 rue de Vaugirard, 75006, tel: 01 43 26 36 36, www.laferrandaise.com*. An old-fashioned red entrance sets the tone for this Left Bank restaurant, with its three atmospheric dining rooms boasting exposed beams and tiled floors. The food is traditional French: try the sardines cooked in lemon juice or the succulent Bresse chicken with morille mushrooms.

Polidor € *41 rue Monsieur-le-Prince, 75006, tel: 01 43 26 95 34*. Open daily for lunch and dinner. This bohemian restaurant is a perennial favourite of students and budget diners. The *plats du jour* have been reliable for around 150 years and arrive in hearty helpings. Blood sausage with mash and rice pudding are just the kind of stodgy dishes to expect. Great value for money.

Le Rostand €€€ *6 place Edmond-Rostand, 75005, tel: 01 43 54 61 58*. This is one of the city's more upmarket cafés, with prices to match – but it's the sort of place you should treat yourself to at least once on a trip to Paris. A fine view of the Jardin du Luxembourg, good cocktails, a delicious snacks menu and an attractive mirrors-and-mahogany interior make this a classy spot for refreshment.

AROUND THE EIFFEL TOWER

Au Bon Accueil €€–€€€ *14 rue de Monttessuy, 75007, tel: 01 47 05 46 11.* Open Mon–Fri for lunch and dinner. What was once a Provençal bistro has been given a total makeover – the décor is now sleek contemporary and elegant, and the menu of classics has been modernised as well. The prix-fixe dinner menu (around €30) is viewed by many locals as one of the best deals in the neighbourhood, and the wine list is excellent. Seats on the terrace have views of its near neighbour the Eiffel Tower.

Le Jules Verne €€€€ *2nd floor, Eiffel Tower, 75007, tel: 01 45 55 61 44.* Open daily for lunch and dinner. Location-wise, this restaurant on the second level of the Eiffel Tower is perfect for a celebration or romantic dinner, though the cooking is not quite as spectacular as the view. Specialities include a *tartare duo* (beef and langoustine), *noix de St-Jacques* (scallops) and *crêpes* with Grand Marnier. One for a special occasion.

MONTPARNASSE

La Closerie des Lilas €€ *171 boulevard du Montparnasse, 75006, tel: 01 40 51 34 50.* Open daily for lunch and dinner. The brasserie still has a lot of charm and richly satisfying fare, though it lives off its reputation as a watering hole in the 1920s – tables are inscribed with the names of clients Lenin, Modigliani and Surrealist poet André Breton. Fittingly, Hemingway's plaque rests on the bar. A pianist plays in the evening. Skip the overpriced restaurant annex.

La Coupole €€–€€€ *102 boulevard du Montparnasse, 75014, tel: 01 43 20 14 20.* Open daily for lunch and dinner. This vast, iconic Art Deco brasserie – the largest in Paris – is still going strong, and has been since 1927. Now run by the Flo Brasserie group, its buzzing atmosphere and popularity remain intact. Brasserie fare includes huge platters of shellfish and grilled meats.

A–Z TRAVEL TIPS

A Summary of Practical Information

A

ACCOMMODATION (see also HOTEL LISTINGS on page 133)

Paris is a popular destination all year round, so booking in advance is always recommended, especially from May to September and during the four annual Fashion Weeks; planning ahead is also beneficial in quieter months, as many establishments offer good discounts or package deals. A complete list of hotels is available from the Paris tourist information office.

For a long stay you might consider renting an apartment. Travel sections of national newspapers carry advertisements; the *International Herald Tribune* and FUSAC (France-USA Contacts), available at expatriate hangouts and embassies, list accommodation for rent. **Alcôve & Agapes** (8bis rue Coysevox, 75018, tel: 01 44 85 06 05, www.bed-and-breakfast-in-paris.com) organise rooms in private homes.

Do you have a single/double room	**Avez-vous une chambre pour une/deux personnes**
What's the rate per night?	**Quel est le prix pour une nuit?**

AIRPORTS *(Aéroports)*

Paris has two main international airports. **Roissy-Charles-de-Gaulle**, 30 km (19 miles) northeast, and **Orly**, 18 km (11 miles) south.

Charles-de-Gaulle to Central Paris

Train: The quickest way of getting to central Paris from Roissy/Charles-de-Gaulle is by RER train. These leave roughly every 15 minutes between 5am and 11.45pm from terminal 2 (take the connecting shuttle bus if you arrive at terminal 1) and run to the Métro stations at Gare du Nord and Châtelet. The journey takes about 45 minutes.

Bus: Roissybus runs between the airport and rue Scribe (near the Palais-Garnier) from terminals 1 gate 30, 2A gate 10 and 2D gate 12. It runs every 15–20 minutes from 5.45am to 11pm and takes 45 to 60

minutes. Alternatively, the Air France bus (to Métro Porte Maillot or Charles-de-Gaulle Etoile) leaves from terminals 2A and 2B or terminal 1, arrival level gate 34. It runs every 12 minutes from 5.45am to 11pm.
Taxis: Can take anything from 30 minutes to over an hour. The charge is metered, with supplements payable for each large piece of luggage; expect to pay in the region of €25.

Orly to Central Paris

Trains: Take the shuttle from gate H at Orly Sud or arrivals gate F at Orly Ouest to Orly railway station. The RER stops at Gare d'Austerlitz, St-Michel Notre-Dame and Musée d'Orsay. It runs roughly every 15 minutes from 6am to 11pm and takes around 30 minutes to Gare d'Austerlitz.
Bus: The Orlybus (to place Denfert-Rochereau) leaves from Orly Sud gate F or Orly Ouest arrivals gate D. It runs around every 10 minutes from 5.35am to 11.05pm. The more expensive **Orlyval** automatic train is a shuttle to Antony (the nearest RER station to Orly). It runs every 5–8 minutes from 6am to 11pm daily, and takes 30 minutes.

Air France buses (to Invalides and Gare Montparnasse) leave from Orly Sud gate J, or Orly Ouest arrivals gate E. They run every 15 minutes from 6am to 11pm and take 30 minutes. Tickets are available from the Air France terminus. See also www.airfrance.fr.
Taxi: The journey from Orly to the city centre takes 20–40 minutes; expect to pay in the region of €20.

B

BICYCLE HIRE (Rental) *(Location de bicyclettes)*

You can hire bikes by the day or week from Paris-Vélo, 2 rue du Fer à Moulin, 75005, tel: 01 43 37 59 22, www.paris-velo-rent-a-bike.fr. Another option is Paris à Vélo C'est Sympa, 37 boulevard Bourdon, tel: 01 48 87 60 01, fax: 01 48 87 61 01, www.parisvelosympa.com.

Alternatively, the Vélib scheme (www.velib.paris.fr) lets you pick up and return one of over 20,000 bikes at any of 1,500 automated 'stations' all over the city. A card valid for a week or a day can be bought from the stations themselves; you then pay for each journey you make, according to its duration.

BUDGETING FOR YOUR TRIP

Generally speaking, prices in Paris are not much lower than those in London, but tickets for cultural attractions and entertainment are usually noticeably cheaper. The cost of getting to Paris in the first place varies widely, depending on season, mode of transport and promotions: a return Eurostar ticket can be had for £59, but if you're flying – especially from outside the UK – the cost can be far higher.

The price of accommodation also varies widely. You can get a double room in a small *pension* for under €50 a night, or you can pay €300 in a luxury hotel. An average price, however, for an en-suite double room in a centrally located, comfortable hotel is around €100–150.

Meals also cover a wide price range, but on average expect to pay around €30–40 for a three-course meal with a half-bottle of house wine. In cafés and bars, a single espresso usually costs in the region of €2, and a 25cl glass of lager about €3. The average entrance price to a national museum or gallery is about €7–8 (municipal ones are free).

C

CAR HIRE (Rental) *(Location de voitures)*

To rent a car you will need your driver's licence (held for at least a year) and passport, as well as a major credit card or a large deposit. The minimum age for renting cars is 25, and you must have held a licence for at least a year. Third-party insurance is compulsory; full cover is recommended. The average daily hire charge for a medium-sized car is around €110.

Among the international car-hire firms operating in Paris are:
Avis, tel: 08 20 05 05 05, www.avis.fr.
Easycar, tel: 01 70 61 85 52, www.easycar.com.

Europcar, tel: 08 25 35 83 58, www.europcar.fr.
Hertz, tel: 01 39 38 38 38 www.hertz.fr.

I'd like to rent a car	**Je voudrais louer une voiture**

CLIMATE

In winter temperatures in Paris average 4°C (39°F); in summer around 22°C (72°F). Spring and autumn tend to be mild, with an average of 11°C (52°F). June, September and October are ideal for visiting, as they are warm, usually sunny, but less stifling than mid-summer.

CLOTHING

Parisians tend to be dressier than Londoners or New Yorkers. In smarter restaurants men may be expected to wear jackets, although ties are rarely insisted upon. Wear decorous clothing at religious sites.

CRIME AND SAFETY

Take the same precautions as at home. There are pickpockets in some Métro stations. Obvious centres of prostitution (such as rue St-Denis and parts of the Bois de Boulogne) are best avoided at night. It's always a good idea to keep a photocopy of your passport in case of theft.

In the event of loss or theft, a report must be made in person at the nearest police station *(commissariat de police)* as soon as possible after the event. This will also be required if you wish to claim from your insurance company. For emergency help, tel: 17.

D

DRIVING

Driving in Paris requires confidence and concentration. Seat belts are obligatory, and the speed limit in town is 50kph (30mph). Do not drive in bus lanes at any time, and give priority to vehicles approaching from the right. This applies to some roundabouts, where cars on the roundabout stop for those coming on to it. Helmets are compulsory for motorbike riders and passengers. Street parking is very difficult to find; spaces are usually metered Mon–Sat 9am–7pm (pay with a Paris Carte, currently €10 or €30 from local *tabacs*); maximum stay is two hours; most car parks are underground (see www.parkingsdeparis.com).

Petrol can be hard to find in the city centre, so if your tank is almost empty head for a *porte* (exit) on the Périphérique (the multi-lane ring road), where petrol stations are open 24 hours a day all year round.

Drivers are liable to heavy on-the-spot fines for speeding and drunk driving. The drink limit in France is 50mg/litre of alcohol in the blood (equivalent to about two glasses of wine) and is strictly enforced.

If you break down, contact Europ Assistance (tel: 08 10 00 50 50) – but expect to pay a high cost unless you have already taken out its insurance cover (www.europ-assistance.co.uk). Other 24-hour breakdown services include Action Auto Assistance (tel: 01 45 58 49 58).

driver's licence	**permis de conduire**
car registration papers	**carte grise**

Priorité à droite	Yield to traffic from right
Ralentir	Slow down
Serrez à droite/à gauche	Keep right/left
Sens unique	One way
Vous n'avez pas la priorité	Give way

E

ELECTRICITY

You'll need an adapter for most British and US plugs: French sockets have two round holes. Supplies are 220 volt, and US equipment will need a transformer. Shaver outlets are generally dual voltage.

EMBASSIES AND CONSULATES

Australia 4 rue Jean-Rey, 75015, tel: 01 40 59 33 00
Canada 35 avenue Montaigne, 75008, tel: 01 44 43 29 00
New Zealand 7ter rue Léonard-de-Vinci, 75016, tel: 01 45 01 43 43
Republic of Ireland Embassy: 12 avenue Foch, 75016, tel: 01 44 17 67 00. Consulate: 4 rue Rude, 75016
UK Embassy: 35 rue du Faubourg-St-Honoré, 75008, tel: 01 44 51 32 81. Consulate: 18bis rue d'Anjou, 75008, tel: 01 44 51 31 02
US Embassy: 2 avenue Gabriel, 75001, tel: 01 43 12 22 22
Consulate: 2 rue St-Florentin, 75001, tel: 08 36 70 14 88

EMERGENCIES *(Urgences)*

Emergency telephone numbers:

Ambulance *(SAMU)*	15
Police *(police secours)*	17
Fire brigade *(sapeurs-pompiers)*	18
From a mobile phone:	112

Police!	**Police!**
Fire!	**Au feu!**
Help!	**Au secours!**

G

GAY AND LESBIAN TRAVELLERS

The city has a large, visible and quite relaxed gay community. Gay bars and clubs are concentrated in the Marais. The magazine *Têtu*, available at kiosks, is a useful source of information.

GETTING THERE (see also AIRPORTS)

By Air: Air France is the main agent for flights to France from the US and within Europe and also handles bookings for some of the smaller operators, such as Brit Air. For British travellers, operators such as British Airways and the low-cost airlines easyJet and British Midland offer flights to Paris from London and other British cities.

By Sea: The following operate from the UK/Ireland: **Condor Ferries** (tel: 0870 243 5140, www.condorferries.co.uk) sail from Weymouth to St Malo and Portsmouth to Cherbourg. **P&O Ferries** (tel: 0870 598 0333, www.poferries.com) sails from Dover to Calais and Portsmouth to Le Havre and Cherbourg. **SeaFrance** (tel: 0871 663 2546, www.seafrance.com) sails from Dover to Calais. **Speed Ferries** (tel: 0870 220 0570, www.speedferries.com) offers a 50-minute crossing from Dover to Boulogne. **Irish Ferries** (tel: 08705 171 1717, www.irishferries.com) runs services from Rosslaire and Cork to Le Havre and Cherbourg.

By Rail: The Eurostar has fast, frequent rail services from London (St Pancras International), Ebbsfleet or Ashford to Paris (Gare du Nord). The service runs about 12 times a day and takes two and a quarter hours (two hours from Ebbsfleet). For reservations, contact Eurostar on tel: 0870 518 6186 (UK) or 08 92 35 35 39 (France) or visit www.eurostar.com. There are reduced fares for children aged 4–11; those under 3 travel free but are not guaranteed a seat.

By Car: Eurotunnel takes cars and passengers from Folkestone to Calais on Le Shuttle. It takes 35 minutes from platform to platform and about one hour from motorway to motorway. You can book in advance with Eurotunnel on tel: 0870 535 3535 (UK) or 08 10 63 03 04 (France) or at www.eurotunnel.com or just turn up and take the next available service. Le Shuttle runs 24 hours a day, all year, and there are between two and five an hour.

By Bus: National Express Eurolines runs services from London (Victoria Coach Station) to Paris daily, providing one of the cheaper ways to get there. For more information contact National Express Eurolines, tel: 0870 580 8080, www.nationalexpress.com, or Eurolines France, tel: 08 36 69 52 52, www.eurolines.com.

GUIDES AND TOURS

Find multilingual guides and interpreters through the Office de Tourisme de Paris *(see page 129)*. For something a little different, try a tour on a Segway, a quirky motorised scooter-style vehicle. See http://citysegwaytours.com/paris for more details.

H

HEALTH AND MEDICAL CARE (see also EMERGENCIES)

EU Nationals: EU nationals can receive emergency medical treatment. You will have to pay, but can claim from the French Sécurité Sociale, which refunds up to 70 percent of your medical bill. You must have a European Health Insurance Card (www.ehic.org.uk).
North American Citizens: In North America, contact the International Association for Medical Assistance to Travellers (IAMAT), 40 Regal Road, Guelph, Ontario N1K 1B5, Canada, tel: 519 836 0102. This is a non-profit-making group that offers members fixed rates for medical treatment from participating physicians. Membership is free, but a donation is requested.

In Paris, English-speaking health services are at the private American Hospital, tel: 01 46 41 25 25, www.american-hospital.org.
Chemists (Drugstores): Pharmacie des Halles, 10 boulevard de Sébastopol, 75004 (Métro Châtelet), tel: 01 42 72 03 23, is open 9am–midnight, Mon–Sat, and 9am–10pm on Sun. Publicis Drugstore, 133 avenue des Champs-Elysées, 75008 (Métro Etoile), tel: 01 47 20 39 25, is open Mon–Fri 8am–2am, Sat–Sun 10am–2pm.

Tap water in Paris is safe to drink.

L

LANGUAGE

Even if your French isn't perfect, your efforts to speak it will be appreciated by Parisians. Do not assume people speak English.

LOST PROPERTY

If you lose your passport, report it to your consulate (*see page 122* or the *Pages Blanches* and *Pages Jaunes* phone books under 'Ambassades et Consulats'; also www.pagesjaunes.fr), as soon as possible.

If your credit card is lost or stolen, the numbers to ring are:
American Express, tel: 01 47 77 70 00
Visa or **Mastercard-Eurocard**, tel: 08 36 69 08 80

To reclaim anything else you have lost, you should go (with ID) to the Bureau des Objets Trouvés, 36 rue des Morillons, 75732 Cedex 15, tel: 08 21 00 25 25 (Métro Convention), open weekdays 8.30am–5pm, except Fri, when it shuts at 4.30pm. You need to visit the office in person, as no information is given over the telephone.

MAPS

Paris Pratique par Arrondissement, an indexed, pocket-sized street-atlas, is the most useful map for visitors. It can be bought for around €6 at newsstands and kiosks. Most Métro stations supply free, decent maps of the Métro system, bus network and RER train system.

MEDIA

Newspapers: The two main national dailies are *Le Monde*, which has a dry, leftish slant, and the more conservative *Le Figaro*. France's biggest-selling daily is *France-Soir*. British, American and other European dailies are widely available on the same day at city-centre kiosks and shops showing *journaux* or *presse* signs.
Radio: France Inter (87.8 MHz) is the main national radio station, with a lot of serious discussion. RTL (104.3 MHz) is the most popular station throughout France, playing music from the charts, interspersed with chat shows.
Television: TF1, France 2, France 3, Canal+, France 5/Arte and M6 are the six main television stations on offer.

MONEY

Currency: The euro (€) is divided into 100 cents (¢ or ct). Coins *(pièces)* come in 1, 2, 5, 10, 20 and 50 cents, and 1 and 2 euros. Banknotes *(billets)* come in 5, 10, 20, 50, 100, 200 and 500 euros.
Banks and currency exchange offices *(banque; bureau de change)*: Take your passport when changing money or travellers' cheques. Your hotel may offer an exchange service, though at a worse rate.
Travellers' cheques: These are widely accepted (with identification).

I want to change some pounds/dollars	**Je voudrais changer des livres sterling/dollars**
Do you accept travellers' cheques/this credit card?	**Acceptez-vous les chèques de voyage/cette carte de crédit?**

OPENING HOURS *(horaires d'ouverture)*

Traditionally, banks open Mon–Fri 9am–5.30pm and close at the weekend, though many now open on Saturday morning and close on Monday. Food shops tend to open early. Traditionally most shops close for lunch, but in Paris, many remain open, closing at 7 or 7.30pm. The larger department stores do not close at lunchtime and are open until 9 or 10pm on Thursday. Most shops close on Sunday.

Are you open tomorrow?	**Est-ce que vous ouvrez demain?**

P

POLICE (see also EMERGENCIES)

The blue-uniformed police who keep law and order and direct traffic are, as a general rule, courteous and helpful to visitors. The CRS

(Compagnies républicaines de sécurité) are the tough guys, brought in for demonstrations. The main police station is the Préfecture de Police, at 9 boulevard du Palais on the Ile-de-la-Cité (tel: 01 53 73 53 73, www.prefecture-police-paris.interieur.gouv.fr).

If you need to call for police help, dial 17 (anywhere in France).

Where's the nearest police station?	**Où se trouve le commissariat de police le plus proche?**

POST OFFICES *(bureau de poste)*

The French post office is run by the PTT (Poste et Télécommunications). Main branches are open Monday to Friday 8am–7pm, Saturday 8am–noon. The central post office, at 52 rue du Louvre, 75001, tel: 01 40 28 76 00, www.laposte.fr, operates a 24-hour service. Stamps *(timbres)* are available at most *tabacs*. Post boxes are yellow.

PUBLIC HOLIDAYS *(Jours fériés)*

Public offices, banks and most shops close on public holidays, though you'll find the odd corner shop open.

1 January	*Jour de l'An*	New Year's Day
1 May	*Fête du Travail*	Labour Day
8 May	*Fête de la Victoire*	Victory Day (1945)
14 July	*Fête Nationale*	Bastille Day
15 August	*Assomption*	Assumption
1 November	*Toussaint*	All Saints' Day
11 November	*Armistice*	Armistice Day (1918)
25 December	*Noël*	Christmas Day

Moveable dates:

Lundi de Pâques	Easter Monday
Ascension	Ascension Day
Lundi de Pentecôte	Whit Monday

T

TELEPHONES *(téléphones)*

Telephone numbers in France have 10 digits. Paris and Ile de France numbers begin with 01; toll-free phone numbers begin with 0800; other numbers beginning with 08 are charged at variable rates; 06 numbers are mobile numbers. There are coin-operated (rare) and card-operated phone boxes in Paris. You get 50 percent more call-time for your money if you ring between 10.30pm and 8am on weekdays, and from 2pm at weekends. A *télécarte* can be bought at various prices from kiosks, *tabacs* and post offices. You can also dial from all post offices. Cafés and tabacs often also have public phones.

UK mobile phones will work in Paris; US ones will not. For long stays, you can buy a pay-as-you-go *(sans abonnement)* mobile phone.

Direct Dialling to Paris from the UK: 00 (international code) + 33 (France) + 1 (Paris) + an eight-figure number. To call abroad from France, dial the international access code (00), then the country code.

Directory Enquiries: 118712 (France Télécom), 118218 or 118000; for a full list of 118 numbers see www.appel118.fr.

Operator: 3123

TIME DIFFERENCES

France keeps to Central European Time (GMT +1 hour; GMT +2 hours Apr–Oct). When it is noon in Paris, it is 6am in New York.

What time is it?	**Quelle heure est-il?**

TIPPING

By law, restaurant bills must include the service charge, usually 12 or 15 percent. Nevertheless, it is common to leave a small additional tip (around 5 percent) for the waiter, if the service has been good. With taxis, it's usual to round up to the nearest euro.

TOURIST INFORMATION *(office de tourisme)*

The main French tourism authority is Maison de la France (23 place de Catalogne, 75014, tel: 01 42 96 70 00, www.franceguide.com). The main Paris tourism authority is the Office du Tourisme de Paris (www.parisinfo.com), whose branches are listed below.

In the UK:

French Travel Centre, 178 Piccadilly, London W1J 9AL, tel: 0906 824 4123 (calls cost 60p per minute), www.franceguide.com. Open Mon–Fri 10–6pm, Sat 10am–5pm.

In the US:

Maison de la France (MDLF), 444 Madison Avenue, NY-10022, tel: 514 288 1904. Also 9454 Wilshire Boulevard, Suite 715, 90212, Beverly Hills, CA, tel: 514 288 1904. Consulate General of France, 205 N. Michigan Avenue, Suite 3770, 60601 Chicago, tel: 514 288 1904, www.franceguide.com.

In Paris:

- 25 rue des Pyramides, 75001. Open daily 9am–7pm, tel: 08 92 68 30 00, www.parisinfo.com
- Carrousel du Louvre, 99 rue de Rivoli, 75001. Open daily 10am–7pm.
- Eiffel Tower, between the east and north pillars. Open May–Sept daily 11am–6.40pm.
- 11 rue Scribe, 75009. Open Mon–Sat 9am–6.30pm.
- 18 rue de Dunkerque, 75010. Open daily 8am–6pm.
- 20 boulevard Diderot, 75012. Open Mon–Sat 8am–6pm.
- 21 place du Tertre, 75018. Open daily 10am–7pm.

TRANSPORT

All public transport in Paris is run by the Régie Autonome des Transports Parisiens (RATP, tel: 32 34, www.ratp.info). There's an information office at 54 quai de la Rapée, 75012 Paris.

Bus *(autobus)*: Bus transport around Paris is efficient, though not always fast. Stops are marked by green and blue signs or shelters.

You can obtain a bus route plan from Métro station ticket counters. Most buses run 7am–8.30pm, some until 12.30am. Service is reduced on Sundays and public holidays. Special Noctambus services run along 10 main routes serving the capital, from 1.30am–5.30am every hour, with Châtelet as the hub.

Bus journeys take one ticket. You can buy a ticket as you board, but it's cheaper to buy a book of tickets *(carnet)* from any Métro station or tobacconist. (Bus and Métro tickets are interchangeable.) Punch your ticket in the validating machine when you get on. You can also buy special one-, three- or five-day tourist passes or the weekly ticket and *Carte Orange (see below)*. Show these special tickets to the driver as you get on, rather than putting them in the punching machine. The fine for being caught without a ticket is €20.

Métro: The Paris Métropolitain ('Métro') is fast, efficient and inexpensive. You get 10 journeys (including connections) for the price of seven with a *carnet* (book) of tickets, also valid for the bus network and – if you stay within Paris and don't go to outer suburbs – for the RER (*Réseau Express Régional,* express lines between the centre of Paris and the suburbs). A special ticket called ***Paris Visite***, valid for one, three or five days, allows unlimited travel on the bus or Métro, and reductions on entrance fees to various attractions. A **day ticket**, *Mobilis*, is valid for the Métro, RER, buses, suburban trains and some airport buses. For longer stays, the best buy is a **Carte Orange** (orange card), valid for unlimited rides inside Paris on the Métro and bus, either weekly *(hebdomadaire)* Mon–Sun, or monthly *(mensuel)* from the first of the month. Have a passport photo ready.

Métro stations have big, easy-to-read maps. Services start at 5.30am and finish around 1am (last trains leave end stations at 12.30am).

Train *(train)*: The SNCF (French railway authority) is fast, comfortable and efficient. The **high-speed service** (TGV) is excellent but more expensive (www.sncf.com or www.voyages-sncf.com).

Validate your train ticket before boarding by inserting it in one of the orange machines on the way to the platform.

Taxi *(taxi)*: Taxis are generally reasonably priced, though there are extra charges for putting luggage in the boot (trunk) and for pick-up at a station or airport. Taxi drivers can refuse to carry more than three passengers. The fourth, when admitted, pays a supplement.

You'll find taxis cruising around or at stands all over the city. You can recognise an unoccupied cab by an illuminated sign on its roof. Fares differ according to the zones covered or the time of the day (you'll be charged more between 7pm and 7am and on Sunday). A fare between Roissy-Charles-de-Gaulle Airport and central Paris might be as much as €40 by day, €50 at night.

The following taxi companies take phone bookings 24 hours a day:

Alpha: 01 45 85 85 85
Artaxi: 08 91 70 25 50
G7: 01 47 39 47 39
Taxis Bleus: 08 25 16 10 10

TRAVELLERS WITH DISABILITIES

Wheelchairs are available to rent from **CRF Matériel Médical**, 153 boulevard Voltaire, 75011, tel: 01 43 73 98 98. **Ptitcar**, www.ptitcar.com, has a fleet of wheelchair-accessible vehicles for transport and tours. They also prepare holiday itineraries for wheelchair users.

Useful Organisations

France: Association des Paralysés de France, Service Information, 17 bvd Auguste Blanqui, 75013, tel: 01 40 78 69 00, www.apf.asso.fr.

UK: RADAR, The Royal Association for Disability and Rehabilitation, 12 City Forum, 250 City Road, London EC1V 8AF, tel: 020 7250 3222, www.radar.org.uk.

US: Society for Accessible Travel and Hospitality (SATH), 347 Fifth Avenue, Suite 610, New York, tel: 212-447 7284, www.sath.org.

V

VISAS AND ENTRY REQUIREMENTS

Nationals of EU countries and Switzerland need a valid passport or identity document to enter France. Nationals from Australia, Canada, New Zealand and the US need passports; South African nationals need a visa. For the latest information, contact your French embassy.

WEBSITES

www.culture.fr official site of the Ministry of Culture
www.magicparis.com travel, shops, hotels, etc
www.meteo.fr the weather
www.monuments-nationaux.fr guide to national monuments
www.pagesjaunes.fr the French *Yellow Pages*
www.paris.org general information on Paris
www.rmn.fr guide to national museum exhibitions

Y

YOUTH HOSTELS

A free guide to French youth hostels is available from the Fédération Unie des Auberges de Jeunesse (FUAJ), 27 rue Pajol, 75018 Paris, tel: 01 44 89 87 27 www.fuaj.org. Tourist information offices offer a booklet entitled *Jeunes à Paris* (Young People in Paris), with details of hostels, student halls and other low-budget accommodation.

Youth hostels are at the following locations:

• **Auberge Jules Ferry**, 8 bvd Jules-Ferry, 75011; tel: 01 43 57 55 60.
• **Auberge Internationale des Jeunes**, 10 rue Trousseau, 75011; tel: 01 47 00 62 00, www.aijparis.com.
• **Centre International de Paris/Louvre** (BVJ), 20 rue Jean-Jacques Rousseau, 75001; tel: 01 53 00 90 90.
• **Le Fauconnier**, 11 rue du Fauconnier, 75004; tel: 01 42 74 23 45.
• **Le Fourcy**, 6 rue de Fourcy, 75004; tel: 01 42 74 23 45.
• **Maubuisson**, 12 rue des Barres, 75004; tel: 01 42 74 23 45.

For further details of Le Fauconnier, Le Fourcy and Maubuisson, see www.mije.com.

Recommended Hotels

This list is divided geographically, covering hotels on the islands and the Right and Left banks. Note that the numbers in the postcode indicate the *arrondissement* (district), eg 75004 is the 4th *arrondissement*.

Hotels on the Islands are small and old-fashioned, and few have lifts. Around the Louvre and Tuileries are some of the city's star addresses, such as the Ritz; further north, on and around the Grands Boulevards, are unassuming establishments with modern amenities. Try Beaubourg, Marais or Bastille for a crop of new boutique hotels.

Western Paris offers full-on luxury in the classic mould. Montmartre hotels, on the other hand, tend to capitalise on the Butte's romantic reputation, but often nakedly angle their rates at the tourist crowd.

On the Left Bank, the Latin Quarter and St-Germain-des-Prés has chic, elegant and traditional establishments, but staying here is rarely cheap. You almost always pay a premium around the Eiffel Tower too. There are a few pleasant addresses to be found in Montparnasse.

The following ranges give an idea of the price for an en-suite double room per night. Service and tax are included; generally, breakfast is not.

€€€€€	over 375 euros
€€€€	240–375 euros
€€€	115–240 euros
€€	65–115 euros
€	below 65 euros

THE ISLANDS

Hôtel des Deux-Iles €€€ *59 rue St-Louis-en-l'Ile, 75004, tel: 01 43 26 13 35, fax: 01 43 29 60 25, www.deuxiles-paris-hotel.com.* Set in a small and attractive 17th-century mansion on the main street of the tranquil Ile St-Louis, this hotel, with just 17 rooms, is comfortable and friendly, with a cellar bar and a vaulted breakfast room with stone walls. Rooms are compact but nicely decorated. Wi-Fi.

Hôtel du Jeu de Paume €€€ *54 rue St-Louis-en-l'Ile, 75004, tel: 01 43 26 14 18, fax: 01 40 46 02 76, www.jeudepaumehotel.com.*

Delightfully set on the pretty Ile St-Louis, this hotel has kept its 17th-century *jeu de paume* (the predecessor of tennis) court. Great for a taste of old Paris and just steps to Notre-Dame. 30 rooms.

Hôtel de Lutèce €€€ *65 rue St-Louis-en-l'Ile, 75004, tel: 01 43 26 23 52, fax: 01 43 29 60 25, www.paris-hotel-lutece.com.* On the exclusive Ile St-Louis, this lovely hotel – which is under the same management as the Deux-Iles *(see page 133)* – has 23 pretty, tiny rooms that are attractive and very quiet. Those on the sixth floor are the most romantic. Wi-Fi access.

THE RIGHT BANK

LOUVRE AND TUILERIES

Hôtel Costes €€€€€ *239 rue St-Honoré, 75001, tel: 01 42 44 50 00, fax: 01 45 44 50 01, www.hotelcostes.com.* This super-hip hotel is just off elegant place Vendôme in this exclusive neighbourhood lined with chic boutiques. The rooms are exquisitely decorated with baroque paintings, heavy drapes and antiques. Some bathrooms have claw-foot bath-tubs and mosaic tiles. Owner Jean-Louis Costes dislikes artificial light, so the hallways are lit with candles; even the beautiful indoor pool is dark. The Café Costes is one of the trendiest places in town. 83 rooms.

Hôtel de Crillon €€€€€ *10 place de la Concorde, 75008, tel: 01 44 71 15 00, fax: 01 44 71 15 02, www.crillon.com.* This palatial, world-renowned hotel forms part of the splendid neoclassical facade that dominates the north side of place de la Concorde. Known for its impeccable service and quality, it also has a celebrated bar and two notable restaurants, Michelin-starred Les Ambassadeurs (headed by chef Jean-François Piège) and the more affordable L'Obélisque. There's also the romantic Winter Garden, for tea, coffee and cocktails.

Henri IV € *25 place Dauphine, 75001, tel: 01 43 54 44 53, no fax, www.henri4hotel.fr.* Some of the least-expensive rooms in Paris can be found at this modest budget hotel that has been popular with visiting students for decades. The excellent location is on the delightful place Dauphine across from Ile St-Louis. The 21 rooms are somewhat old-fashioned, with shared bathrooms. Only a short walk from Notre-Dame and St-Michel. Reserve well in advance. No credit cards.

Ritz €€€€€ *15 place Vendôme, 75001, tel: 01 43 16 30 30, fax: 01 43 16 31 78, www.ritzparis.com.* One of the most prestigious addresses in the world, the Ritz has been associated with the rich and famous for over 100 years. Rooms are plush, decorated in Louis XV style with antique clocks and rich tapestries; many have fireplaces. The spa has a beautiful indoor pool; there are two fine restaurants, the famous Hemingway bar and a pleasant garden.

GRANDS BOULEVARDS

Hôtel Chopin € *46 passage Jouffroy, 75009, tel: 01 47 70 58 10, fax: 01 42 47 00 70, www.hotelbretonnerie.com/chopin.htm.* Set at the end of an historic 19th-century glass-and-steel-roofed arcade, this is a quiet, friendly, simply furnished hotel. A fabulous price for the location. Book well in advance to stand a chance of staying in one of the 36 rooms.

Hotel Claridge €€€–€€€€ *37 rue François-1er, 75008, tel: 01 47 23 54 42, fax: 01 47 23 08 84, www.hotelclaridgeparis.com.* A small boutique hotel offering the personal touch at decent rates in the stylish district lying between the Seine and the avenue des Champs-Elysées. The rooms are attractively furnished with antiques. No restaurant.

Hôtel Edouard VII €€€–€€€€ *39 avenue de l'Opéra, 75002, tel: 01 42 61 56 90, fax: 01 42 61 47 73, www.edouard7hotel.com.* Historic, family-owned hotel on one of the grandest avenues in Paris, just a stone's throw from the Palais Garnier and the Louvre. Some rooms at the front have balconies with marvellous views of the opera house. The hotel features the swish Angl'Opéra restaurant *(see page 109)* and a smart, comfortable bar.

Four Seasons George V €€€€€ *31 avenue George V, 75008, tel: 01 49 52 70 00, fax: 01 49 52 71 10, www.fourseasons.com/paris.* One of the most prestigious addresses in Paris, just off the Champs-

Elysées. The George V offers the height of opulence, with beautifully classic rooms with modern touches and magnificent marble bathrooms. Exquisite service, and a fabulous spa.

Plaza Athénée €€€€€ *25 avenue Montaigne, 75008, tel: 01 53 67 66 65, fax: 01 53 67 66 66, www.plaza-athenee-paris.com.* This palatial hotel, with lavish Versace decor, has soundproofed rooms, a club, restaurant and suites furnished in Louis XVI or Regency style. Super-chef Alain Ducasse is in charge of the restaurant *(see page 109)*. If you can't stretch to the price of a room, treat yourself to a cocktail in the fashionable bar.

BEAUBOURG, MARAIS AND BASTILLE

Hôtel Bourg Tibourg €€€ *19 rue du Bourg-Tibourg, 75004, tel: 01 42 78 47 39, fax: 01 40 29 07 00, www.bourgtibourg.com.* Situated on a charming narrow street in the heart of the Marais, this 17th-century building is home to a well-kept, affordable boutique hotel. Rooms are warmly decorated with cheery yellow or red wallpaper. Breakfast is served in a vaulted dining room with exposed stone. 31 rooms.

Hôtel Duo €€€ *11 rue du Temple, 75004, tel: 01 42 72 72 22, fax: 01 42 72 03 53, http://duo-paris.com.* Excellently located trendy hotel in the Marais. Rooms are furnished in the contemporary style, with good-sized bathrooms. There's a bar downstairs, and a gym.

Pavillon de la Reine €€€€ *28 place des Vosges, 75003, tel: 01 40 29 19 19, fax: 01 40 29 19 20, www.pavillon-de-la-reine.com.* This romantic, mid-sized hotel, located on the beautiful place des Vosges, feels like a country château. Rooms vary greatly in size and price, but most have four-poster beds, exposed wooden beams and antiques. There's also a cosy lobby bar with evening wine-tasting, and manicured gardens.

Hôtel de la Place des Vosges €€€ *12 rue Birague, 75004, tel: 01 42 72 60 46, fax: 01 42 72 02 64, www.hotelplacedesvosges.com.* An intimate, carefully renovated hotel in a former stables with only 16 rooms. It's popular and in a great location, so book ahead.

Hôtel St-Merry €€€ *78 rue de la Verrerie, 75004, tel: 01 42 78 14 15, fax: 01 40 29 06 82, www.hotelmarais.com.* One of the most unusual hotels in Paris and once a 17th-century presbytery. Rooms have stained-glass windows and are decorated with mahogany church pews and iron candelabra and, in one, a carved-stone flying buttress. The phone booth is in a confessional. A Gothic masterpiece.

WESTERN PARIS

Hôtel Keppler €€€€ *10 rue Keppler, 75016, tel: 01 47 20 65 05, fax: 01 47 23 02 29, www.keppler.fr.* Some of the best accommodation for the price in this posh neighbourhood. The 49 rooms are large and furnished comfortably; four have balconies. There is a spiral staircase, welcoming fireplace and a bar with room service. An impeccably managed, family-owned hotel.

MONTMARTRE

Hôtel Ermitage €€ *24 rue Lamarck, 75018, tel: 01 42 64 79 22, fax: 01 42 64 10 33, www.ermitagesacrecoeur.fr.* This small hotel is located close to Sacré-Cœur in an old residential neighbourhood. An excellent budget choice, with friendly staff and colourful bedrooms decorated in French farmhouse style. There's a lovely courtyard and terrace, where breakfast is served in summer. 12 rooms. No credit cards.

THE LEFT BANK

LATIN QUARTER AND ST-GERMAIN-DES-PRÉS

Abbaye St-Germain €€€ *10 rue Cassette, 75006, tel: 01 45 44 38 11, fax: 01 45 48 07 86, www.hotel-abbaye.com.* This 17th-century abbey, attractively situated between the Jardin du Luxembourg and St-Germain-des-Prés, has been beautifully adapted into a hotel. The charm of the old decor has been maintained – some of the 46 rooms have beams – but there are all mod cons. Lovely garden too. A favourite haunt of writers and artists. Staff are helpful and attentive.

Hôtel d'Angleterre €€€ *44 rue Jacob, 75006, tel: 01 42 60 34 72, fax: 01 42 60 16 93, www.hotel-dangleterre.com.* The location couldn't be better, on a quiet, upmarket street lined with art galleries. This lovely hotel was the site at which the Treaty of Paris, proclaiming the independence of the US, was signed in 1783; in the 19th century it was used as the British Embassy. Ernest Hemingway lodged here (in room 14) in 1921. Rooms are fairly small and furnished with antiques; only the top-floor doubles are spacious. Delightful terrace and garden.

Hôtel Familia €€ *11 rue des Ecoles 75005, tel: 01 43 54 55 27, fax: 01 43 29 61 77, www.hotel-paris-familia.com.* Within a few minutes' walk of the islands and St-Germain-des-Prés, the Familia offers solid comforts in smallish rooms for a modest price; rooms on the fifth and sixth floors have views of Notre-Dame. Another attraction for the hotel's many regular guests is the hospitable Gaucheron family who live on the premises and take pride in every detail. Look out for the frescoes painted by a local artist. 30 rooms.

Hôtel des Grandes Ecoles €€–€€€ *75 rue du Cardinal-Lemoine, 75005, tel: 01 43 26 79 23, fax: 01 43 25 28 15, www.hotel-grandes-ecoles.com.* At first glance, you might think you were in the French countryside here. There are 50 large, prettily furnished rooms around a cobbled courtyard and garden of established trees and trellised roses. Although it is a short uphill walk from the Métro, you are still near enough to attractions including rue Mouffetard.

Hôtel de Nesle € *7 rue de Nesle, 75006, tel: 01 43 54 62 41, fax: 01 43 54 31 88, www.hoteldenesleparis.com.* A laid-back students' and backpackers' hotel. Facilities are basic, but bedrooms are cheerfully decorated with murals, furnished to various eclectic themes and spotless. There is also a garden with a pond and an impressive palm tree.

Hôtel Le Sainte-Beuve €€€ *9 rue Sainte-Beuve, 75006, tel: 01 45 48 20 07, fax: 01 45 48 67 52, www.hotel-sainte-beuve.fr.* On a quiet street, steps from the excellent shops on rue d'Assas and a short walk from the Jardin du Luxembourg. The rooms are tastefully furnished, with air-conditioning; those on the top floor have skylights in the bathrooms and romantic views over the rooftops.

AROUND THE EIFFEL TOWER

Amélie €€ *5 rue Amélie, 75007, tel: 01 45 51 74 75, fax: 01 45 56 93 55, www.hotelamelie-paris.com.* A short walk from the Eiffel Tower, this small, friendly family-run hotel has some of the lowest rates in the area. Renovated rooms have small refrigerators and private bathrooms. A narrow wooden staircase leads up to the four levels of rooms; there's no lift. Breakfast is served in the small lobby.

Bourgogne et Montana €€€ *3 rue de Bourgogne, 75007, tel: 01 45 51 20 22, fax: 01 45 56 11 98, www.bourgogne-montana.com.* A lovely hotel in a building dating from 1789, tucked away behind the Musée d'Orsay. The 30 or so modern, spacious rooms are good value for this pricey neighbourhood. The large doubles are worth the extra splurge and come with double basins as well as antiques.

Hôtel Lenox €€€ *9 rue de l'Université, 75007, tel: 01 42 96 10 95, fax: 01 42 61 52 83, www.lenoxsaintgermain.com.* This trendy hotel is decorated in Art Deco style and is very popular among style-conscious types. There's a bar, and the rooms are spotless. Reserve well in advance.

Hôtel Verneuil €€€ *8 rue de Verneuil, 75007, tel: 01 42 60 82 14, fax: 01 42 61 40 38, www.hotelverneuil.com.* Lovely hotel in an elegant 17th-century building in the upmarket 7th *arrondissement*, with small but attractive rooms in the traditional style. Discreet service. Singer Serge Gainsbourg lived on this street, and the wall outside his old house is decorated with graffiti in homage. Well placed for St-Germain.

MONTPARNASSE

Hôtel Aviatic €€ *105 rue de Vaugirard, tel: 01 53 63 25 50, fax: 01 53 63 25 55, www.aviatic.fr.* A comfortable small hotel on a pleasant street not far from the Luxembourg Gardens. The bedrooms have been recently refurbished, and there is a charming breakfast room and Empire style lounge. Worth upgrading to a superior room, if your budget allows.

INDEX

Berlitz pocket guide

Paris

Sixteenth Edition 2010

Written by Martin Gostelow
Updated by Simon Cropper
Series Editor: Tony Halliday

Printed in Singapore by Insight Print Services (Pte) Ltd, 38 Joo Koon Road, Singapore 628990. Tel: (65) 6865-1600. Fax: (65) 6861-6438

Photography credits
AKG London 20, 60; Apa 4bc, 81, 98; The Art Archive 89; The Art Archive/Musée du Louvre 39; Pete Bennett 53; Corbis 24; Kevin Cummins 4tl, 4bl, 5tl, 5tr, 38, 42, 50, 76, 82; Jerry Dennis 5bc, 8, 10, 18, 27, 28, 29, 30, 32, 33, 36, 41, 45, 49, 59, 62, 64, 65, 67, 69, 70, 72, 74, 77, 79, 85, 87; Annabel Elston 14, 58, 71; Courtesy of the French Embassy 22; Jay Fechtman 17, 26; Tony Halliday 86; Francisco Hidalgo/Getty 35; Britta Jaschinski 11, 12, 40, 44, 46, 49, 51, 52, 54, 56, 68, 78, 90, 92, 93, 94, 101, 102, 105, 106; Musée Association Les Amis d'Edith Piaf 97; Ilpo Musto 48
Cover picture: 4Corners Images

Contact us

At Berlitz we strive to keep our guides as accurate and up to date as possible, but if you find anything that has changed, or if you have any suggestions on ways to improve this guide, then we would be delighted to hear from you.

Berlitz Publishing, PO Box 7910, London SE1 1WE, England.
fax: (44) 20 7403 0290
email: berlitz@apaguide.co.uk
www.berlitzpublishing.com

M RER T
Paris
RATP
32 46 • wap.ratp.fr
www.ratp.fr
Asnières–Gennevilliers Les Courtilles
Les Agnettes
Gabriel Péri
Saint-Ouen
Mairie de Clichy
Porte de Clichy
Carrefour Pleyel
Mairie de St-Ouen
Garibaldi
Porte de St-Ouen
Guy Môquet
La Fourche
Brochant
de Clignan
Lamarck Caulaincourt
Abbesses
Blanche
Pigalle
Place de Clichy
Pont de Levallois Bécon
Anatole France
Louise Michel
Porte de Champerret
Pereire–Levallois
Pereire
Wagram
Malesherbes
Rome
Villiers
Liège
La Défense
Grande Arche
Esplanade de La Défense
Pont de Neuilly
Les Sablons
Porte Maillot
Neuilly–Porte Maillot
Monceau
Europe
Trinité d'Estienne d'Orves
St-Georges
Notre-Dame de-Lorette
Courcelles
Gare St-Lazare
St-Lazare
Haussmann St-Lazare
Ternes
St-Augustin
Chaussée d'Antin La Fayette
Argentine
Porte Dauphine
Charles de Gaulle Étoile
Miromesnil
St-Philippe du-Roule
Havre Caumartin
Opéra
RoissyBus
Avenue Foch
Victor Hugo
Kléber
George V
Franklin D. Roosevelt
Auber
Quatre Sep
Madeleine
Pyramides
Boissière
Alma Marceau
Champs Élysées Clemenceau
Palais Royal Musée du Louvre
Louvre Rivoli
Avenue Henri Martin
Rue de la Pompe
Iéna
Concorde
Trocadéro
Pont de l'Alma
Invalides
Tuileries
Musée d'Orsay
Pont Neuf
La Muette
Passy
La Tour Maubourg
Assemblée Nationale
Boulainvilliers
Champ de Mars Tour Eiffel
Solférino
Varenne
Bir-Hakeim
École Militaire
Rue du Bac
St-Germain des-Prés
Ranelagh
Avenue du Pdt Kennedy
Saint François Xavier
Sèvres Babylone
Mabillon
St-Sulpice
Dupleix
La Motte Picquet Grenelle
Vaneau
Jasmin
Avenue Émile Zola
Rennes
Duroc
St-Placide
Notre-D des-Cha
Michel-Ange Auteuil
Porte d'Auteuil
Église d'Auteuil
Javel
Cambronne
Ségur
Montparnasse Bienvenüe
Mirabeau
Javel André Citroën
Charles Michels
Commerce
Falguière
Vavin
Sèvres Lecourbe
Michel-Ange Molitor
Chardon Lagache
Pasteur
Gare Montparnasse
Edgar Quinet
Boulogne Jean Jaurès
Exelmans
Pont du Garigliano
Félix Faure
Gaîté
Volontaires
Bd Victor
Boucicault
Marcel Sembat
Porte de St-Cloud
Boulogne Pont de St-Cloud
Lourmel
Vaugirard
Pernety
Balard
Convention
Plaisance
Billancourt
Porte de Versailles
Pte de Vanves
Pont de Sèvres
Issy Val de Seine
Corentin Celton
Porte d'Orléans
Malakoff Plateau de Vanves
Malakoff Rue Étienne Dolet
Issy
Mairie d'Issy
Antony
Châtillon–Montrouge
Propriété de la RATP - Agence Cartographique - PMI 07-2009- CC Design: bdcconseil - Reproduction interdite

Basilique de St-Denis
13 St-Denis–Université
CDG
B
St-Denis–Porte de Paris
La Courneuve Aubervilliers
La Courneuve 8 Mai 1945 7
Le Bourget
La Plaine Stade de France
Fort d'Aubervilliers
Aubervilliers–Pantin Quatre Chemins
Bobigny Pablo Picasso
12 Porte de la Chapelle
Pantin
Simplon
Jules Joffrin
Marcadet Poissonniers
Marx Dormoy
Porte de la Villette
Bobigny–Pantin R. Queneau
Corentin Cariou
Église de Pantin
E
Funiculaire de Montmartre
Château Rouge
Crimée
Barbès Rochechouart
La Chapelle
Riquet
Ourcq
Porte de Pantin
Hoche
Anvers
Stalingrad
Laumière
Gare du Nord
Jaurès
Danube
Pré St-Gervais
Mairie des Lilas
Magenta
Louis Blanc
Bolivar
11
Poissonnière
Château Landon
Botzaris
Gare de l'Est
Colonel Fabien
Buttes Chaumont
Cadet
Belleville
Pyrénées
Jourdain
Place des Fêtes
Télégraphe
Porte des Lilas
Château d'Eau
Jacques Bonsergent
Strasbourg St-Denis
Couronnes
Saint-Fargeau
Goncourt
Grands Boulevards
Bonne Nouvelle
Temple
République
Ménilmontant
Pelleport
Arts et Métiers
Oberkampf
Père Lachaise
Porte de Bagnolet
Gallieni
Réaumur Sébastopol
Sentier
Parmentier
3
Filles du Calvaire
Rue St-Maur
Gambetta
Mairie de Montreuil
9
Châtelet Les Halles
St-Sébastien Froissart
Philippe Auguste
St-Ambroise
Croix de Chavaux
Rambuteau
Hôtel de Ville
Richard Lenoir
Voltaire
Alexandre Dumas
Chemin Vert
Bréguet Sabin
Robespierre
St-Paul
Charonne
Maraîchers
Porte de Montreuil
Châtelet
Bastille
Avron
Rue des Boulets
2
Buzenval
St-Michel Notre-Dame
Pont Marie
Ledru-Rollin
Faidherbe Chaligny
A
Cluny La Sorbonne
Sully Morland
6 Nation
Pte de Vincennes
St-Mandé
Maubert Mutualité
Gare de Lyon
Quai de la Rapée
Reuilly–Diderot
Cardinal Lemoine
Jussieu
Montgallet
Picpus
Bérault
1
Place Monge
Gare d'Austerlitz
Bel-Air
Port-Royal
Daumesnil
Château de Vincennes
Censier Daubenton
10
Michel Bizot
orlybus
Dugommier
Denfert Rochereau
Saint Marcel
Les Gobelins
Bercy
Porte Dorée
St-Jacques
Campo Formio
Quai de la Gare
Cour St-Émilion
Porte de Charenton
Place d'Italie
Corvisart
Chevaleret
Liberté
Glacière
5
Nationale
Bibliothèque Fr. Mitterrand
14 Olympiades
Charenton–Écoles
Tolbiac
Cité Universitaire
Maison Blanche
Porte d'Italie
Porte d'Ivry
Pierre et Marie Curie
École Vétérinaire de Maisons-Alfort
Ivry sur-Seine
Maisons-Alfort–Stade
Le Kremlin Bicêtre
Porte de Choisy
Maisons-Alfort Les Juilliottes
Gentilly
Villejuif Léo Lagrange
T 3
Mairie d'Ivry 7
Vitry sur-Seine
Créteil–L'Échat
Orlyval tarification spéciale
Villejuif Paul Vaillant-Couturier
Créteil–Université
Orly
Villejuif Louis Aragon 7
C
D
8 Créteil–Préfecture

Berlitz®

www.berlitzpublishing.com

BERLITZ PHRASE BOOKS

The Perfect Companion for your Pocket Guides

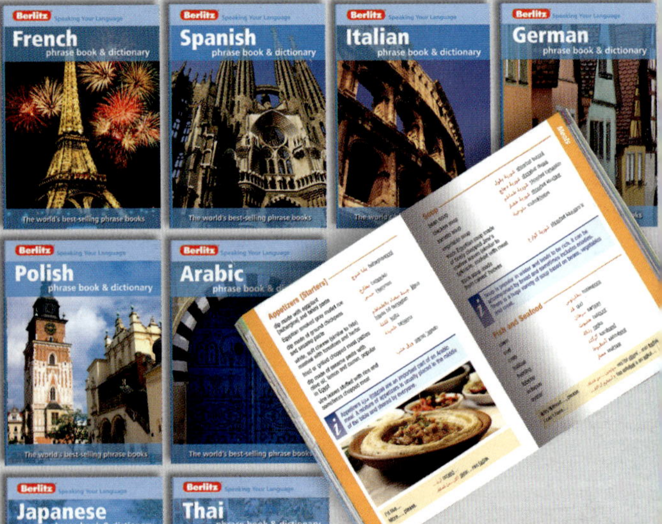

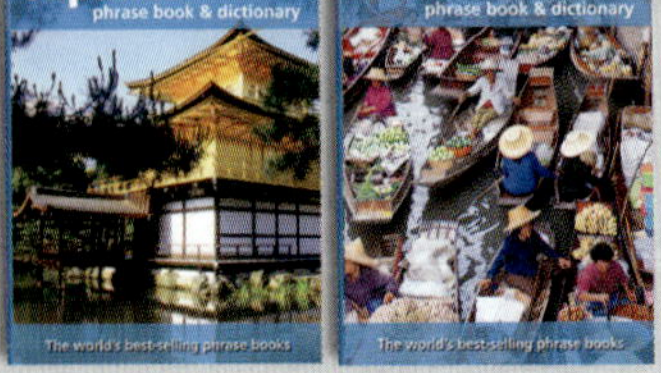

Speaking Your Language

Available in more than 30 languages, including Mandarin Chinese, Danish, Hindi and Hungarian